TEXT BY
ALBERT GOLDMAN

PHOTOGRAPHS BY
DOUGLAS AND LENA VILLIERS

DESIGNED BY BEA FEITLER

CARN
IN

IVAL
RIO

HAWTHORN BOOKS, INC.
Publishers · New York
A Howard & Wyndham Company

To Charlotte, Daniel, and Nicky
(D.V.)

For Jane Krupp: truest of friends, brightest of wits
(A.G.)

The black-and-white photos which decorate the text are archival and documentary pictures from approximately 1910 to 1950. We would like to thank Diana Bethlem; the Cultural Office of the Brazilian Embassy in Washington, D.C.; Fabiano Canosa; RioTur; *O Globo*; and Museo da Imagem e do Som for their assistance and kind permission to use these photographs.

Introduction

I first came to Rio in 1974, with my wife Lena and a few friends at the invitation of Jorge Guinlé, one of Rio's most fabulous characters, party-giver and dedicated socialite. We initially planned to stay for about ten days to get some winter sunshine and see the Carnival. After the first few days of attending pre-Carnival balls and going to an endless round of parties given by Rio's social set, we started to get restless and decided to set off on our own to photograph the Carnival. The London we had left behind us was in the grip not only of snow, gray weather and rain, but was also beset by one of our periodic economic crises. Rio was a revelation of optimism—beaches packed with suntanned bodies, crowds dancing the samba on street cafe tabletops, the city alive to its nerve ends with a feeling of elation and anticipation. We were so thrilled by the excitement of the city, its people and their mad Carnival that we came back each year for the next three years; the photographs in this book are the result of those visits. Following the second trip, Lena and I put together a portfolio of photographs. Over the previous few years I'd scoured the bookshops of Rio, London, New York and Paris and found very few references to Carnival except for a few pictures and brief articles in travel books about Brazil. The time seemed right for a full-length, well-illustrated book on the vast urban psychodrama that is Rio Carnival.

An old friend suggested that I approach Albert Goldman, an excellent writer on pop culture, to produce an extended essay on Carnival, as pictures alone would not convey the full story. As it happened, he, too, had been a dedicated visitor to Rio Carnival since 1971 and he was enthusiastic about the opportunity to write text for a book about it (he had covered Carnival for *Life*, *Travel & Leisure*, and *Esquire*. In 1977, he was invited down as a guest of honor of the Mayor of Rio, Marcos Tamoyo.) Albert, Lena and I set off once again for Rio and its pleasures: Albert to research and start to write his essay, Lena and I to take more photographs. We didn't really want to illustrate Albert's text, nor could we expect him to write a commentary around our photographs. We went largely where our cameras led us and photographed people and places that "had" to be photographed, took pictures of things that happened impromptu, mainly because of the impact they had on us rather than because they were absolutely fundamental to the overall story. During Carnival, everything happens simultaneously—events peripheral to the parades, the official Carnival, tend to be sporadic and spontaneous. It is difficult to know where to be at any one time, and we tended, therefore, to be where we thought there would be the most fun. Many of our pictures are not strictly, perhaps, entirely representative of the totality of Carnival, but what we did record is a personal reaction.

I particularly want to thank my wife, Lena, for her invaluable help while I was putting the book together. She started off as my assistant, organizer and travel agent; learned to take photographs while we were in Rio and finished up taking a large number of the photographs in the book, including the cover shot. My thanks also to Bea Feitler, originally from Rio, now living and working in New York, who designed the book. Finally my thanks to our many helpers and friends in Rio who drove us around, interpreted and pointed us in the right direction generally.

Douglas Villiers

"Many peoples have been used to observe an annual period of licence, when customary restraints of law and morality are thrown aside, when the whole population give themselves up to extravagant mirth and jollity, and when the darker passions find a vent which would never be allowed them in the more staid and sober course of ordinary life."

—Sir James Frazer, *The Golden Bough*

Carnival in Rio

There's no rhythm in the world like the beat of that Carnival samba down in Rio. It grabs you the moment you check into your hotel, seizes you when you least expect it, hanging up a neatly pressed suit or sipping a quiet Scotch or burrowing gratefully into cool, white sheets. *Boom-dah! Boom-dah! Rat-daddy-ah-dah-yattity-duh-to-duh!* Up from the street, the funky black asphalt, it bounces: a hypnotic bass drum endorsed with a savage syncopation of tin shakers and Afro cowbells and rasping scrapesticks.

You leap out of bed and stare down into the street. There you see your first Carnival swarm, the first melee of closely packed revelers, with arms upraised in abandon, heads thrown back with blissful smiles, mouths open singing the strident samba song, while knees bend, feet shuffle, and hips roll erotically in a grandly inviting strut. Roped round with a ship's thick hawser, they look like a slave gang gone berserk, jumping joyously in its shackles.

In the days that follow this first flash, you'll see that street samba blown up to colossal proportions. You'll hear that same raggedy-assed tin-can rhythm thundered out by three-hundred-piece percussion bands that sound like jungle apocalypses. You'll see that gaggle of jean- and *tanga*-clad kids transformed into stunningly costumed, carefully choreographed chorus lines that stretch for miles on end. You'll see those quivering thighs and arched up *bundas* (the ass is the focal point of Brazilian culture) enlarged to heroic proportions, as the biggest, hottest, meat-shakin'-on-the-bone mammas in the world get it on for the folks back in Amazonia. You'll glut yourself on so much authentic black culture that when you get back home to New York, Tokyo, or Düsseldorf, you won't want to hear no more talk about soul, funk, glitter, disco, Afro, or *jigabuono*. Carnival at Rio is not only the grandpappy of all these fads and fashions—it is their *archetype*: the ultimate fulfillment of William Blake's prophetic proverb, "Exuberance is Beauty."

Beauty and exuberance are the keynotes of Rio itself, the tropical metropolis *par excellence*. Though the Cariocas seem intent on destroying Rio's fabled beauty with their nitwit enthusiasm for the cockroach Volkswagen and the phallic glass and metal condominium tower, the marvelous city transcends all its distractions. The loveliness of Rio's beaches, lagoons, mountains, rain forests, and pastel-colored nineteenth-century houses; the excitement of its streets, teeming with open-air markets, loud-mouthed vendors, restless shopping crowds; the beguilement of Brazilian popular music which, with the pop music of England and the United States, has taught the whole modern world how to celebrate itself in song; the sensual allure of the sexy Brazilians in their skimpy *tangas* and campy Carnival costumes; the chic, swank air of the nightclubs, restaurants, discotheques; the romantic quality of the nightscape, the unforgettable image of city lights reflected in the Lagoon or the stunning view from the mountains of Tijuca toward the eerily illuminated Christ statue atop Corcovado and beyond to the Sugarloaf and down to Botafogo and Guanabara bays, a carpet of glittering gems swept into the grand curves of the scalloped shoreline—this cornucopia of fascinating imagery and sensory enchantments is reason enough to go flying down to Rio at any time of year.

During Carnival, however, Rio is not simply beautiful or picturesque or moodily romantic: it is ebullient and delirious; ecstatic and explosive; fantastic and hallucinatory. The whole vast city has cut loose from its moorings in work, order, self-restraint, and morality. It is a giant bacchanal, an orgy, with every Carioca intent on just two things: exhibiting himself to the height of his notoriously narcissistic self-esteem or seeking with insatiable appetite every delight of food, drink, drugs, sex, and excitement that the resources of one of the richest, most sophisticated and hedonistic cities on earth can provide.

While the whole city parties, several hundred thousand of its poorest citizens labor to launch a vast theatrical enterprise. Having spent virtually the entire year in preparation and rehearsal, they now present the greatest show on earth, a show of shows that has cannibalized over the years every entertainment offering of the modern presentation theater; from the Mardi Gras to the Rose Bowl, from the Ziegfeld Follies to the Busby Berkeley musicals, from the Day-Glo garishness of the Ice Capades to the awesome psychedelic pageantry of Federico Fellini. Not Max Reinhardt at his most *kolosal* nor Roxy at Radio City Music Hall nor Samuel Goldwyn nor Cecil B. DeMille at the height of Hollywood's megalomania ever dreamed of staging a spectacle as vast and costly as Rio's annual all-night parade of samba clubs. Imagine a fifteen-million dollar extravaganza with a cast of forty thousand —all singing, all dancing, all bursting with the pent-up passions of a whole year's anticipation of this one supernal moment! You could pile up every Las Vegas show ever presented and stash them all in one little corner of Rio's supershow. Were you to try to do with paid professionals in the United States what is done every year in Rio with amateurs who shoulder the cost of their own show, the budget would be a couple of hundred million dollars— for one night's fun! Not since ancient Rome has any people ever exhibited such a mad devotion to the philosophy of *circum et panem* as have the Cariocas. Indeed, in Rio you can skip the bread, but never the circus.

Rich as these inducements sound, they are surpassed, at least for the philosophic observer, by the other facets of this extraordinary festival. For one thing, Carnival is the greatest psychodrama ever staged. In an age that has increasingly dedicated itself to the substitution for religion of spontaneous rites of confession, purgation, and self-absolution, no spectacle could be more absorbing than the sight of an entire society rushing out into the streets to reveal in unmistakable words, songs, rhythms, gestures, dances, rituals, and lavishly designed pageants and masquerades precisely what lies closest to its heart. The Brazilian word for a Carnival costume is *fantasia*. That says it all. When the Carioca dons his costume, he steps into his fantasy, he becomes his fantasy, he *lives* his fantasy!

The most common Carnival fantasy is the exotic erotic. Rio rhymes with Eros all year round, as the population strolls to the neighborhood beaches day in and day out virtually naked (the string bathing suit, with its frank avowal of the ass, made its first appearance on the sands of Ipanema), speaking a body language that is all sighs, swoons, and sloe-eyed enticements. If there is a sexier race on the planet than the Cariocas, the urgent science of erotology does not know them. While the more advanced nations drift toward the ambiguous ideal of a third sex comprised of men who are increasingly feminine and women who are rapidly becoming masculine, Rio maintains the traditional sexual polarities in all their electric arcing-sparking force.

The Girl from Ipanema remains, as ever, the perfect fulfillment of the physical ideal of the mid-twentieth century. Her exquisitely slender, tubular, space-age body, with its attenuated legs, virginally budding breasts, and racy curves, stretched out, supplely supine, as if squeezed from a human-sized tube of suntan cream onto the sands of the surfer's beach—where like some maritime creature, she first digs her burrow, the two neat holes for her heels, the bigger socket for her flawlessly rounded butt, and the little bump for her goggled head—is one of the natural wonders of the modern world: perhaps the very first item on the What To Do on Earth List carried aboard every passing UFO.

When Carnival sends its inciting jungle drums echoing down the hills and out onto the beaches, this normally languid and lazy creature, whose life is measured by her endless applications of suntan oil (which transforms her skin into a precious kind of human leather), her three daily baths, her late-afternoon naps, and her bimonthly visit to the depilatory salon (where her pubic hair is coated with paraffin and wrenched from her body), is roused suddenly to a strange frenzy. Suddenly, she aspires to be a superstar, a sex queen, a Liza Minnelli, Gina Lollobrigida, or Raquel Welch. Exchanging her bathing *tanga* for one no less skimpy but bedizened with sequins and her bra for a couple of pasties, she becomes a Carnival bacchante, flinging her arms into the air and proclaiming with her every gesture not "Take me!" but "Look at me! Want me! Raise me by the force of your lust to the height of my own self-infatuation!"

While the Girl from Ipanema is starring in her personal spectacular, other less glamorous but comparably motivated revelers are preparing to enact their most cherished erotic dreams. As in most countries where Carnival is a deeply rooted institution, the rule in Rio is that during the festival husbands and wives, girl friends and boyfriends, may part company so that each can fulfill himself without the inhibiting presence of the other. The wealthy man sends his wife and family to some delightful beach or mountain resort, while he remains in the city to "entertain foreign clients." The sophisticated society matron, separated (but never divorced) from her industrialist husband, holds a grand party at her elaborately terraced house, climbing the side of a thumbs-up volcanic mountain, where she surrenders her sixty-three-year-old body, tucked and stitched by Rio's celebrated plastic surgeons into a semblance of 23, into the arms of several pungent-smelling drummers from the slums of the northern industrial districts. In these raw factory belts, which are the heartland of the samba, the poor folk simply split up for the week. As one slum bum confided with a wicked leer: "All year long I flirt with my best friend's girl. Then, Carnival weekend—I catch her!" On the Saturday afternoon before Ash Wednesday, the outlying beaches are covered with couples enjoying sex in the sand. On the nights of the great parades, the overwrought *sambistas*, kept waiting for hours in the dark streets before they "go on," relieve their feelings in erotic encounters that soon transform the asphalt into an extravagantly costumed tribal orgy.

Another even more important fantasy-confession made during Carnival concerns that great triad of existential values: race, wealth, and power. Contrary to what is often said, Brazil is a profoundly racist society. Conquered by a tiny number of white Europeans, who were determined to exploit an entire continent, Brazil was populated from earliest times by the systematic practice of miscegenation. The result is, as a common expression puts it: "Nothing is harder to find in Brazil than a person who is all white or all black." The corollary of this extraordinary racial confusion is a refinement of the sense of race—and a sensitivity to the stigma of color—that would astound the color-blind inhabitants of North America or the racially blasé populations of Europe or Japan. Brazilians are so abnormally conscious of color gradations that their language is incredibly rich with words that define with a stock breeder's precision the exact amount of black or white in any given human being.

The dark end of the spectrum commences with *preto* (pure black) and *cabra* ("goat" or near-black); then comes *cabo-verde* ("Cape Verde," meaning lighter black but with straight hair, thin lips, and narrow, straight nose) and *escuro* ("dark one" but lighter still); next is *mulato escuro* (dark brown), *mulato claro* or *pardo* (light brown), followed by *sarará* (light skin but "bad," kinky hair), the *moreno* (light skin and straight hair but with a tinge of Negro visible only to the trained eye), and the *branco de terra* or *branco de Bahia* ("white of the land"), whom none but a Brazilian would dream of calling anything but white; finally, the scale ends with the pure-blooded whites, who are divided into brunette and blond. Oh, to be blond in Brazil!

With this extraordinary emphasis upon race (which mingles with the notions of wealth and power, as in the proverb "Money whitens"), nothing lies closer to the hearts of Brazil's black, brown, and beige populations than the desire to be beautiful, aristocratic, rich, and *white*. The simplest *fantasia* is a near-naked body painted from head to toe with chalk. The steps up the ladder of prosperity from this cheap body paint to the modest cost of a Hawaiian hula skirt to the expense of a Carmen Miranda costume to the opulence of a Lillian Russell gala with train to the wealth and ostentation of the full regalia of her Imperial Majesty, the Empress of Brazil—surrounded by train-bearers, fan-wavers, canopy-carriers, and throne-porters—are infinite in their number and variety. However costumed the Negro is at Carnival, one thing is clear: As he struts down the boulevards in his plumes and finery, he is experiencing for one night the heady thrill of belonging to the master race.

Though the masquerade of Carnival is designed to give the poor domestic servants and factory workers a taste of white power, particularly as it was wielded during colonial times, when a man's position in society was as plain as the ruffles round his wrist or the gold chain round his neck, the spectacle serves even better as a device for releasing the Negro's essence as an African. Overwhelmingly, the themes of Rio's great Carnival pageants are glorious assertions of black power. A samba club comprising two or three thousand people, most of them descendants of slaves, will take a theme from Brazilian history and inflect it into a great ode of praise for the Negro and his contributions to Brazil. The pageant will first reflect upon and revive what the Negro was in Africa. The ancient tribes, the Yorubas, Haussas, Minas, Gêges, Mandingos, Zulus, Jolofas, Cabindas, Ambaquistas—will be summoned up again, with their grass and textile costumes, primitive fetishes and looming idols. They will come flooding down the gaudily decorated avenues at 3:00 A.M., dancing and singing and shouting to the sound of deep-throated tribal drums. They will so gorge and stretch the spectator's senses, memory, and associational capacity that the effect will be literally sublime.

To an American enthusiast for black culture, accustomed all his life to seeing black people play, dance, sing, and express themselves in every fashion, the sight of these great black pageants comes like a vision of the archetypal patterns in Plato's heaven. "Here it is at last!" you exclaim. "After a lifetime of thrilling to the black arts, of contemplating the black soul, of seeking with ever-deepening understanding the indwelling essence of Afro-American culture, I have discovered finally its single greatest expression. These drums, chants, cries, bodies, faces, smiles; these dazzling, barbaric colors and patterns—gaudy, flaunting feathers and fabrics, glinting with metal and flashing with glass—what are they?" Why, nothing less than *the total exfoliation of the black man's imagination in the New World.*

That's reason enough to send me flying down to Rio.

What Is Carnival?

Carnival is an ancient Christian festival whose meaning could be summed up in the phrase "Feast today, for tomorrow we fast." Carnival immediately precedes Lent; hence the word *carnival* derives from two Latin roots: *carne* (meat) and *levare* (to take away, as from the table). According to the rationalizers of the church calendar, the merry-making and licentiousness of the festival—the masquerades, pageants, processions, and horseplay—are just a final fling, a last taste of self-indulgence before the season of penance and self-denial that precedes the commemoration of the Savior's death and resurrection.

This official explanation, however, leaves a great deal unexplained. For one thing, the orgiastic intensity of the festival seems excessive for the occasion. What's more, the typical features of the celebration—the violence, the sexual licentiousness, and the paraphernalia of impersonation—are totally at odds with the ethos of Christianity. The first modern anthropologists to study this festival drew the irresistible conclusion that here, as in so many other instances, the Christian festival is merely an overlay designed to disguise and rationalize an earlier pagan festival which the church despaired of ever stamping out and chose instead to paper over.

The festival in the ancient world that bore the closest resemblance to Carnival was the great Roman holiday of Saturnalia: the celebration of the reign of Saturn, the first god and ruler of the world during the Golden Age. A holiday of universal mirth, jollity, and sexual license, Saturnalia was one of a number of festivals in the ancient world that derived from that basic ritual of primitive societies: the fertility rite.

To grasp the meaning of fertility rites, one must realize that primitive man did not possess the faith of his civilized descendants that after every winter there will be a spring. Primitive man believed that the universe was an animate creature, much like himself, subject to decline and decay, to attrition and death. Consequently, he feared that unless he exerted himself and put forth his powers to revive nature, the world might run down and die before his eyes. The principal means that primitive man employed for assuring the continuing fecundity of the earth and the energy of the sun and heavenly bodies was imitative magic. By setting nature an example of sexual energy—archetypically, by performing coitus en masse in a tribal orgy—primitive man believed the earth and sun would be roused from their annual torpor and inspired to bring forth the crops and flocks of previous years.

Just as important as the orgy is the other great theme of the Roman holiday: the inversion of the master-slave relationship. Wrote the celebrated anthropologist Sir James Frazer, "No feature of the festival is more remarkable. Nothing in it seems to have struck the ancients themselves more than the licence granted to slaves at this time. The slave might rail at his master, intoxicate himself like his betters, sit down at table with them, and not even a word of reproof would be administered to him. Nay, more, masters actually changed places with their slaves and waited on them at table." As in ancient Rome, so in modern Rio: As the maids and car washers strut the boulevards in the regalia of queens and kings, the society belles at the most exclusive balls offer themselves like whores, while the masters of Brazil prowl about dressed like beach bums.

This drastic overturning of the social order is the very essence of Carnival. Once a society has reached the point where the classification of people into masters and slaves makes no sense, the animating tension of Carnival collapses and the festival becomes a vestigial remnant. One observes this in all places where Carnival was once a great local tradition: Venice, Vienna, Munich, the Rhineland, Southern France, and even New Orleans. These prosperous, advanced, democratic societies lack the necessary social polarities: a class of industrial serfs, desperate to escape their thralldom and a jaded, decadent upper class eager to experience the *frisson* of being whores or bravos or transvestites exhibiting themselves before a jeering mob, like a degenerate Caesar playing the fool in the Colosseum. Only in Brazil can still be found the social conditions and traditions necessary for a classic Carnival.

Rio Carnival cannot be explained by the reasons given in guidebooks: the Portuguese tradition of the *entrudo*—the missile-hurling Carnival revel—or the ecclesiastical tradition of great costumed processions or even the characteristic Brazilian disposition toward merrymaking. Rather, the flourishing of Carnival is explained by the more fundamental fact that the Brazilians, despite their panache of Third World industrial-technological progressiveness, as symbolized by the Martian landscape of Brazilia, are still at bottom a nation of planters and peons, of plutocrats and proles. It is this age-old social structure with its tensions, frustrations, fantasies, and cravings for release that really sustains and inspires Rio Carnival, making it another Saturnalia: the topsy-turvy orgy of the masters and the slaves.

The Escolas de Samba

At the base of Rio's social pyramid lie the poor blacks who inhabit the *favelas*, the "shantytowns," perched on the bald summits of Rio's volcanic hills or extended precariously into Guanabara Bay, tottering on rickety piles and rotting planks. At a distance the spill of tile roofs and whitewashed walls tumbling down the side of the mountain is picturesque, even charming. Close up the *favela* is a nightmare of urban poverty, a hodgepodge of walls barely able to maintain decency, slops running along open ditches, the air full of children's cries and the strident blare of television sets. The stench is unforgettable.

The inhabitants are the poorest of the immigrant workers who have been flooding into Rio ever since the boom years of World War II. Ostensibly employed as hod carriers, stevedores, factory hands, maids, nurses, and launderers, many of the *favelados* are in fact idle for most of the year: Their days are spent scratching about for enough to eat and to burn; their nights in the universal recreations of the slums—partying, drinking, playing games of sex and love. Their brief, hectic lives are cursed with as many social ills as physical diseases. They are victims both of racketeers and the police. In recent years the Brazilian government has been dismantling the slums and moving the *favelados* out of the city into distant suburbs where they are housed in blank-faced concrete housing projects or in rows of common-wall company houses that resemble barracks. The people of the *favelas* fight vigorously these evictions because the little they gain in terms of sanitation and structural solidity is more than offset by the costs of rent and the loss of easy access to work.

No one in his right mind would associate the ideas of art or culture with this rabble of deracinated peasants. Yet these "culturally deprived" urban peons have created out of their own dreams and aspirations, out of their occasional glimpses of film and daily exposure to television—plus the self-sacrifice entailed in allotting a considerable portion of their meagre incomes to the expenses of Carnival—one of the most impressive popular cultures to be found anywhere in the world today. There is nothing like it in the slums of North America, nor can it be matched by any other Latin-American nation—or, for that matter, most other cities of Brazil. Rio, and Rio alone, is the seat of those absolutely unique institutions: the *escolas de samba,* the samba schools or Carnival guilds.

A samba school is a hierarchically ordered, protocol-laden, fanatically team-minded social club in the slums. In the old days the schools and the *favelas* were one; even to this day some of the greatest schools, like Mangueira, are based on squatter's land amid a steeply pitched pile of shanties. It would be a mistake, however, to identify the great schools with the *favelas* because over the course of years outstanding schools have developed far from the hills in industrial suburbs or outlying dormitory towns. What's more, the greatest schools have attained such prestige that today they draw their membership not only from the neighborhoods in which they originated but from other far more affluent districts and classes. Today, there are approximately 1,000 schools and *blocos* (less prosperous, less highly organized clubs) in Rio.

Four great samba schools have in recent years monopolized the attention of the public: Portela, Mangueira, Salgueiro, and Imperio Serrano. Of the four, the most famous and influential is unquestionably Portela, the blue and white, a school that has probably contributed more to Rio Carnival than any other force in the history of the event.

Portela commenced its colorful history about fifty years ago as a spontaneous association of what were then called *"bambas,"* (or "big men of the samba"). The word *bamba,* which used to turn up with monotonous frequency in Carnival songs but is now going out of style, was once interpreted to this writer by Antonio Carlos Jobim, Brazil's greatest composer of bossa novas and the composer of the score for *Black Orpheus.* Jobim, who is one of those rare composers whose knowledge of language and sensitivity to its use rivals his command of tones, pointed to the common Brazilian expression, *corda de bamba* (or "tight rope") as the root of the concept. "To walk a tight rope" is a very common phrase in Brazilian Portuguese, and its ordinary meaning is very much the same as it would be in English. As picked up and developed in the slums, however, the expression became equivalent to a word that was once common to underground American English—"hipster."

The hipster was the hero of the black American slums of the thirties and forties. He was typically a jazz musician or hanger-on in that world. A man of cool control, practical address, knowledge of the streets and their forbidden pleasures, he was above all else an existential hero who was "hipped"—that is to say booted to the hip like a fisherman in deep, cold, rushing water, armed with protective knowledge of all possible situations and contingencies and thereby proof against anything which life could offer or aim at him. The *bamba,* being Latin and explosive, is not quite the cool hipster, but the *bamba,* like the hipster, is a shrewd, adroit, adept slum hero who is remarkable for his ability to walk the wire—to adjust himself on the spur of the moment to the sudden and unpredictable challenges of the street life.

Back in the twenties when the modern samba was first coming to the fore in Rio, the leading *bambas* of various *blocos* used to gather at the house of a Baianese lady whose name was Ester Maria da Cruz, but who was known in the short-circuited lingo of the slums as Dona Ester. Playing, singing, dancing, partying together at Dona Ester's, a certain group of men became the nucleus of a new club, which was formed in 1923 and given the characteristic name, *Vai Como Pode* ("Make It Any Way You Can")—an offhand, idiomatic, supercool and casual phrase bent ironically backward against the passions and intensities that such groups felt and engendered among their members and audiences. One of the universals of slum language both in North and South America is the habit of treating everything that is important, passionate, and transcendental as if it were trivial, casual, and of merely ephemeral interest. This is the profound irony of the so-called counter-culture, which was not invented in the sixties by white kids in the streets of Berkeley but which grew with the force of a glacier (or a disease) over the course of many generations from the deepest centers of black culture in both hemispheres. Counter-culture is quite literally a negation of conformist culture, the culture of the ruling class; hence it expresses itself most naturally in the language of inversion, in irony, in all its senses, linguistic, musical, spiritual and in terms of what the middle class calls "antisocial behavior," "delinquency," "sociopathic personality," and so on.

Among the *bambas* who founded Make It Any Way You Can, were two men who for many years guided the destiny of the school. Paulo Benjamin de Oliveira, known to fame as Paulo da Portela, was a bootblack by trade. Paulo belonged to the first generation of *sambistas*, men born around the turn of the century and reaching their maturity during the twenties, at which time the samba emerged as the most characteristic music of Rio. A composer and orator of local renown, Paulo earned the title "Civilizer of the Samba." His principal achievement was the introduction of language that was elegant and "difficult" into the typically colloquial lyrics of the samba: the sort of language that is always envied and admired by the illiterate people of the slums, with their overweening belief in the power of the word.

To appreciate Paulo Portela's innovations, you have to understand first what a simple little ditty the samba was in his day. In 1929, when the first samba school appeared on the streets of Rio, it sang the following verses, which are typical of the old street samba:

> Poor girl, so foolish and smitten,
> So conceited in her mindless talk,
> Hiding her pride, in vain she tries to win my love.

Such simple sentiments in such plain language were not for Paulo Portela. One of his best-known sambas is an ode to Copacabana Beach. The beach has been marked off traditionally into sections that correspond with the old lifesaving stations, which were numbered Post One, Post Two, etc. commencing at Leme and running down to *Postos Seis* at the far end near Fort Copacabana. The most beautiful moment of the day in this district is the sunrise, when the horizontal light of dawn comes glancing across the water like liquid fire or lambent gold. Reflecting on such a morning in the forties, Paulo composed the following tribute:

> The strand is rippling like a golden flame,
> Rims buildings as a landscape in a frame
> Of English grace.
> The crystal ocean in unruffled calm
> Reflects the noble lineaments and charm
> Superb of Post Six.

What is so delightful about this little ode is first of all the choice selection of stock phrases and fondled clichés which the poet has assembled like a magpie the objects of her nest. Words like "strand" and phrases like "crystal ocean" are knocked out of the hands of educated poets like sticky sweets from the palms of children. To the slum poet such phrases are a sign of education and literary ability. They show how much the culture of the slums is simply the culture of the ruling classes fifty years ago—a prime example of cultural lag. Another amusing feature of the poem is the image of the building along the shore rimmed by the sea in a "frame of English grace." Obviously this is a recollection of a rare trip to an art gallery, where the bootblack caught a glimpse of some nineteenth-century English landscape painter: a diverting enough conjunction of cultural incongruities. What makes the poem a perfect marvel of unconscious humor, however, is the conclusion, which deserves to be enshrined in a textbook under the heading "Bathos." Where could you find a finer example of what Alexander Pope called "The Art of Sinking"? As the poet reaches the climax of his evocation, he closes his eyes, concentrates his mental gaze, fixes on the "noble lineaments and charm superb" of the shore-front prospect and then murmurs the words, *"Postos Seis"*—precisely the language one would use to direct a taxi driver. The fact is, of course, that in the slum world of Paulo da Portela, *Postos Seis* was a phrase like "Park Avenoo" in the lyrics of the American thirties: a phrase that connotes class, privilege, and distinction. For his auditors, this phrase achieved its purpose, concluding the poem "High on a Peak in Darien"—a slum sublimity.

A more important figure than the "Civilizer of the Samba" was its principal politician, the legendary Natal, born into this world as Natalino José de Nascimento. Natal was for so many years the prime mover and principal benefactor of Portela that when he died in 1975 it must have seemed as if one of the greatest chapters in the history of the Carnival had closed. Indeed, the accounts one hears of his huge funeral and the attention devoted to his demise in the press show that like the school he fostered, Natal had grown over the course of a long life from a mere "numbers man" in the slums to something like a national hero and benefactor. Reviewing his life and character is perhaps the simplest and best way to understand how the samba schools came into existence.

The first and most important thing about Natal was his vocation: Throughout his mature years he was the king of Rio's notorious numbers game, the *jogo de bicho* or "game of the animals." This game, which corresponds to the policy game of the American slums, is a simple form of gambling based on a number published every day all over Rio. Each number corresponds to one of twenty-five animals in a complicated arrangement that allows for combinations and parlays. Instead of saying you are betting this or that number, you say you are betting "the eagle" or the "rabbit." The

game is operated by an immensely wealthy and politically influential Mafia that allots the territories and resolves the disputes of the rival *bicheiros*. To the poor worker in the slums, the game is enormously important, because it represents his one chance to get rich and to enjoy for a few days or weeks the luxurious life of which he dreams. The ultimate dream is to hit on the numbers just before Carnival; then to appear before one's friends and neighbors in a magnificent *fantasia*.

Trading in dreams and frustations, it was highly appropriate that Natal should have developed as a great realizer of his people's most cherished wishes. Unlike most racketeers, who swallow up the money they make in self-indulgence, Natal aspired to the patriarchal role. He not only financed his samba school but donated large sums to the building of athletic and recreational facilities in Madureira and Oswaldo Cruz, the lower-class commercial districts where he operated his business. A power, a potentate, an uncrowned king of the blacks, Natal was an ostentatiously casual figure. His standard costume was pajamas and wooden clogs, with a straw hat, sunglasses, and a big cigar stuck in his mouth. A scholarly looking old godfather, he ruled his people with carelessly uttered obscenities and offhand gestures. His favorite oath was "jizzum!"

Natal got into the *jogo do bicho* in 1928, just three years after the accident that marked him for life. An employee of the old Central Railroad of Brazil, he had been running after a moving train when he slipped on the platform and fell under the wheels. His right arm was deeply cut but not severed. It was gangrene that compelled the doctors to amputate the limb. Unemployed after his recovery and virtually unemployable, he snapped at the first job to come along. It was a very dangerous post in the *jogo do bicho*.

The local boss of the game was fighting for his territory against a tough gang called the Turkish Brothers. These Lebanese hoodlums had gunned down a number of his street bankers and were winning the war when Natal came along. The boss told Natal that he didn't care whether he had one arm or two. What he wanted was a man of absolute courage. If Natal were brave, he would become rich. "When I heard him say those words, I shivered," recalled Natal forty years later. "I always wanted to be rich so that I could help everybody, build churches, and make my club." The bicho boss handed Natal two .45s. He said, "I'm going to send you to Turiaçu, where the Turkish Brothers have got rid of many of my men. Let's see how you make it."

Natal proved to be tougher than the Turkish Brothers; in fact, over the course of a long life, he proved to be absolutely invulnerable. "I never had a bullet in my body," he once remarked, "but I've had more than a hundred fired at me. That's why they say my body is 'shut'." Within a few years, he had secured the territory and reached the point where he could walk around without his .45s, doing business just on the strength of his word. He was on his way not only to becoming rich and powerful but to becoming king of the slums.

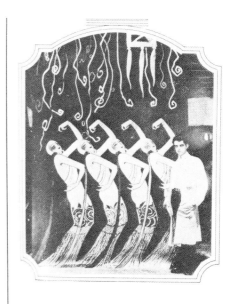

It was at this point that he fell in with Paulo Portela and the *sambistas*. Samba in those days was a sporting event, just like football. The *sambistas* were tough street fighting men who would dress up like *Baianas*, but under their skirts they would pack a knife, a razor, or a gun. Their favorite place of assembly was the *Praça Onze de Junho*, a little park in the heart of the Mangue red light district: a maze of narrow streets, evil-looking houses and bad-assed babies of both sexes. Probably a lot tougher than the Basin Street tenderloin in New Orleans where jazz was born.

Nobody had heard the term *samba school* in those days. On the big boulevards of the central city, the prosperous people and the decent working-class families paraded in organizations called *ranchos* and *grandes sociedades*. The former were costumed marching groups, both men and women, predominately white; the latter were society people who would ride huge and elaborately sculptured floats in torchlight parades that were written up the next day in all the papers. The *sambistas* jumped in *blocos:* compact little masses of dancers who all wore the same costume. The *blocos* were comprised entirely of bullies and bravos from the slums. Their encounters with other *blocos* from neighboring districts would end invariably in bloody fights in which many were injured or killed. Naturally, the *sambistas* were not very popular with the police, and for many years their name was anathema to the city government.

In 1929 a *bloco* named *Deixa Falar* ("Let 'em Talk") emerged as the first *escola de samba*. The peculiar phrase they employed to distinguish themselves from the *blocos* was the result of their meeting regularly near a local normal school. From saying over and over again, "Let's get together tonight at the Escola" (and perhaps from a certain pretension to being "professors" of samba), they adopted for their type of organization the high-falutin' title of "School of Samba." It was also a good way to throw dust in the eyes of the police.

Having organized themselves under a fancy title, they began to ape the manners of their betters. They borrowed from the *grandes sociedades* the practice of leading the school with a rank of horsemen blowing fanfares (a practice soon dropped). They borrowed from the *ranchos* such conventional devices as the school banner and the *destaques* (literally, "standouts"), those elaborately costumed figures that resemble human effigies. The success of the first appearance of *Deixa Falar* was the signal for the creation of many other *escolas de samba*. In 1930 five new schools turned out to compete at the *Praça Onze*, including Natal's outfit *Vai Como Pode* and *Estação Primeira* ("First Station"), from the hill of Mangueira, then the first station on the Central Railroad. In 1931 the city government recognized the schools as a special category of Carnival club and required their registration. It was

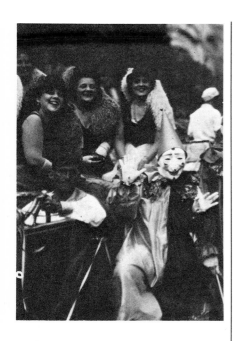

at this time that a bureaucrat turned up his nose at the name, Make It Any Way You Can. "Can't you call yourself something better?" he demanded. "Where is your clubhouse?" "On the Rua da Portela," he was told. "Well, why not call yourselves Portela?" And Portela it was and is and shall be until the last drum is beaten and the last samba danced.

Though the early samba schools were rough and ready outfits with no more than a hundred members and very little money, they had one great thing going for them: the samba. The rhythm had been introduced into Rio, probably from Bahia, around the turn of the century; but it only caught on during World War I. The first samba ever recorded (in 1913) is still pungent with the flavor of those early days, when the samba was just a sarcastic slum shout, banged out on a tin can and sung with the impudence of urchins and rowdys. Titled *"Pelo Telephone"* ("On the Telephone"), this primitive piece is so purely a product of the street that it is difficult to translate. Basically, it is a series of discontinuous verses that jump all over the place. First we hear that the "master of revels" has called on the phone and left this message: "Don't worry about anything—go out and have fun playing Carnival." Then the song jumps to a shame-on-you verse: "I hope you pay for what you've done, steal another's lover, then go make a [voodoo] enchantment." Finally, in the manner of all pop dance crazes, the samba gets around to extolling itself and the marvelous effects of its rhythm: "If the little bird doesn't have what it takes, that's because she never danced the samba. The samba makes you shiver, makes you weak, but it also gives you joy!" Samba will be analyzed later; the point to mark here is simply that the music has always had a distinctly lower-class black flavor, like the blues or the boogie-woogie in America. The decent working folk and the middle and upper classes always marched and partied to the rhythms of the Brazilian march, which is a long way from Strauss or Sousa but nothing like the huckster-voiced samba.

These class distinctions are, as we shall see, very basic to the history of Carnival. The whole modern development of this great cultural phenomenon can be seen as the struggle of a raw lower-class culture to push its somewhat decadent rivals, both in song and pageantry off the streets. The history of the samba is very much, therefore, like the history of black music in America. After decades of being scorned by even its own people, the samba has gradually come to dominate the national culture until now there is hardly any other kind of Brazilian music—except white exploitations of black music—to be heard in the popular media.

On the boulevards, samba and the schools had a hard fight for many years. Gradually, however, the *sambistas* picked up influential supporters, especially in the press. From being consigned to the whorehouse neighborhood of the *Praça Onze*, they graduated over a period of years to the foremost avenues of the city. In 1957 the parades were transferred to Avenida Rio Branco and soon after to Rio's grandest and broadest avenue, the Presidente Vargas. In this quarter of a century, the whole structure and character of the schools was transformed. From being loose little slum clubs, they became elaborate and hierarchical organizations, bound by stiff regulations, staffed with pompously titled officials, and stuffed with thousands of members. At this point it might be well to pause for a moment to sketch in the organization and rules of the samba schools.

According to Brazilian law, every samba school must have a charter or constitution setting forth the regulations that govern the organization. This charter must be registered with the civil registry of the local municipality. It is customary for a school to have a president, a first and second secretary, a first and second treasurer, and as many as seven vice-presidents, each one in charge of a different department of the school, such as social activities, public relations, rehearsals, music, band equipment, and sports activities. The school may have as many as four distinct governing bodies: the general assembly, the board of directors, the deliberative council, and the financial council.

The general assembly meets twice a year or whenever conditions demand the judgment of the entire membership. The meetings of these bodies have often been compared with the deliberations of the Brazilian Parliament. The language is courtly and the speeches long winded. The _sambistas_ are pleased to have the opportunity to air their views and exercise their tongues. Anybody who is familiar with the rhetoric of the slums in any major city will be able to imagine the impassioned exhortations and vainglorious exhibitionism that attends these interminable confabulations.

The real work of managing the school is performed by the board of directors, which is staffed by the vice-presidents or directors responsible for each of the school's departments. Though Carnival is the prinicipal business of a samba school, there are year-round social activities that demand constant planning and attention by these officials.

Strictly speaking, a school is a federation of little clubs that are called _alas_, or "wings." The _alas_ collect their own dues, arrange their own parties, dinners, and picnics, and when Carnival season nears they negotiate with their school for the part they wish to play in the grand pageant, choosing a costume pattern according to the state of their finances and practicing their steps at regularly scheduled rehearsals. The school, for its part, operates the _terreiro_, or "practice stadium," where the rehearsals and large social affairs are held; it also furnishes such indispensable elements as the percussion band, or _bateria_, the wings of composers and Baianese women, the standard bearers, the solo dancers, the _destaques_ ("standouts," the wearers of the most elaborate and costly costumes) and the prodigious bureaucracy of directors and minor officials.

Typically, the president of a big samba club will be the boss of the local numbers game. The clubs spend enormous sums on their annual pageants, and without the support of the criminal underworld, it would be impossible for them to mount such costly productions, even though they do earn considerable amounts by charging admission to public rehearsals, making deals with record companies and TV networks, as well as receiving substantial contributions from local merchants and fans. The biggest clubs receive subsidies from the municipal government, but these public funds amount to very little indeed.

Preparations for Carnival

One month after the old Carnival ends, preparations commence for the new Carnival. In March, which is autumn in Rio—when temperatures are moderate and the normal business life of the city revives—the schools begin to confer on the strategy they will adopt for winning at the next Carnival. What is at stake is a small amount of money, a gold statue that bears a close resemblance to the American film industry's Oscar, and a great deal of honor—the ultimate value in any Latin society. The competition between the oldest schools now reaches back half a century; and while it no longer entails the pitched battles with knives and guns that once characterized these annual encounters, it is still rife with the brutal passions and the cunning trickery of the slums. No Carnival is complete without its scandal. There must always be a near disaster at the last, most critical moment, as the president of a school is suddenly thrown into jail on information provided by another school or the newspapers reveal that the judges may have been bribed or that some sly saboteur has crept into the holy of holies—the storeroom where the school's vast array of drums is kept—and slashed the goatskins stretched painstakingly over the head of every instrument.

The first decision a school must make every year is what should be the theme of its pageant. Carnival is as rigorously controlled as are professional athletic events in the United States. (Indeed, it parallels in many ways that other great Brazilian passion —soccer.) The book of Carnival regulations is thick and constantly being interleaved with new rules. The most basic rule of all is that no pageant must ever be staged with a political theme. Once, years ago, a patriotic samba club produced a pageant commemorating an obscure war with Paraguay that provoked an international incident. Since that time political themes have been strictly verboten. Nor is Carnival exempt from the censorship that is exercised in Brazil over every medium of communication from the press to pop songs. In fact, ever since the days of Brazil's great dictator, Getulio Vargas (who ruled intermittently from the thirties until his suicide in 1954), the ideal theme for a Carnival pageant has been some nice, safe, politically innocuous subject—the balloon ascents of Brazil's colorful aviation pioneer, Santos Dumont; or some legendary bay in Bahia; or, perhaps, a humorous tribute to the national cuisine. Such themes provide plentiful opportunites for colorful pageantry, they have a vaguely patriotic and pedagogic cast, and above all, they do not offend the powers that be.

The selection of themes would be a very arbitrary exercise of taste were it not for the rule of fashion. *La mode* is a dictator every bit as strict and compelling as are the generals in Brazilia. Every year there is always some one idea that has occurred to everyone, apparently, at the same time. In the early seventies the typical pageant was a tribute to the Negro. Africa was all the rage and any excuse for summoning up the tribal imagery of the Dark Continent was abundantly welcome. Recently, the vogue has changed. Now the hip thing is to produce a tribute to the Old Rio or the Old Carnival, often with humorous or mock-heroic imagery.

When a samba school chooses a theme, after long and earnest deliberation, the next thing it does is order its wing of composers to embody this theme in a *samba enredo*, or Carnival samba. Those who know the samba only in its sophisticated, top-forty bossa nova form have no idea of the real thing. Like soul, rhythm and blues, or boogie-woogie, the samba is a classic product of Afro-American culture. Its characteristic beat, especially when delivered with the immense power of a three-hundred-piece percussion band, evokes simultaneously the imagery of a jungle ritual and a hard-driving, steam-hissing locomotive chugging up a steep grade. Poised perfectly at the center of contemporary sensibility, midway between the primitive and the futuristic, the natural wilderness and the industrial wasteland, evoking the ecstatic frenzy of the tribe and the mindless ecstasy of the machine, the samba is one of those incredibly potent rhythmic germs that can sprout an entire world. First comes the beat, then the feet, then the voices, the poetry, the pageantry, the life-style, and finally the hero of this world, the *bamba*, or samba big shot. Eventually, you have a vast beat-inspired culture covering an entire continent as swing covered America in the thirties or rock covered the western world in the sixties.

The true samba, the pure samba, is a very rudimentary kind of music, employing only those resources most characteristically African: drums and voice. The drums can be multiplied to infinity, the voices can be enlarged to a half-mile procession of several thousand people singing in unison, but the samba remains unalterably the same: a simple monodic chant with percussion. The melodic idioms employed by the samba composers range from the ebullient, square-cut O-le-le, O-la-la football tune to the more insinuating, Latin-flavored, very Rio de Ja-nay-rho sort of melody to the only style that, in my opinion, cuts the mustard: the minormoded, low-pitched, darkly colored, tumultuously passionate strain, reminiscent of the dark throbbing melodies of the gypsies, that comes tumbling out of the singers' mouths with all the force of a desperate confession. Laced with authentic African words and punctuated with timeless tribal shouts, this splendidly somber samba appears at least once every year to remind its listeners of the vast burden of pain and suffering that is the basic experience of Brazil's immense population of former and present slaves.

Sad to say, the quantity and quality of music composed each year for Carnival is declining drastically. In the heyday of Carnival music—the heyday of popular song all over the world, the thirties—melancholy marches, tricky maxixes, and sprightly sambas poured from Brazilian composers' pens. Several hundred songs were published in time for each year's celebration, many of them becoming enduring classics, like "Yes, We Have No Bananas" or "Brazil" or "*Mama, Eu Quero*," tunes that are played every year at the balls or over the radio or in the little seaside bars where young people gather to make merry in the late afternoon. This delightful music, especially the erotically melancholic marches, which were the original Carnival music, before the take-over of the samba and the samba schools in the forties, was the product of a white, middle-class Brazilian Tin Pan Alley that boasted some brilliant composers, like the legendary Noel Rosa, the Cole Porter of Brazil, and the marvelously Gallic show tune writer Lamartine Babo. The faceless black composers of the current generation are not so gifted or accomplished as their predecessors. Like the hacks who grind out soul and disco music in America, they lean so heavily on the clichés of their idiom that most Carnival sambas today sound like products of a plastic extrusion mold. When you switch on the radio, you are saddened to hear on most stations not the richly distinctive musical language of Brazil but dreadful imitations of American music or simply the straight sound of Detroit, New York, Memphis, and LA. Cultural imperialism, the global triumph of cars, Cokes, and cowboys, commences with the invasion of those flying saucers, the LP records.

When a samba school commissions a *samba enredo* on a particular theme, it does not anticipate that the forty, fifty or sixty song writers and lyricists that comprise its wing of composers will produce just one song. Ten, twenty, or thirty songs is the more likely result of a month of intensive creative effort that begins with library research and concludes with the songs being tested by the school's *puxadores de samba*, literally, "samba pullers" because, with the sound of their amplified voices they pull the long train of the samba school up the boulevard.

The best songs are printed on little slips of colored paper and distributed at the weekly dances held at the school's clubhouse. All through the rainy months of the Brazilian winter, the *sambistas* try out the new tunes to see which one has the greatest appeal. Finally, one samba is chosen as the theme song of the year's pageant. From that moment on, all the considerable resources of the school are bent toward making this song flesh.

A scenographer is engaged to design the pageant. He hires sculptors, costume designers, seamstresses, electricians, mechanics—the whole crew of a Broadway musical. As these professionals labor to build the floats, sew the costumes, and wire the sound systems, the dance directors put the *alas* through their paces, the officials of the school put their heads together to find the money for all this costly activity, and the membership begins to dream of the great night, when, as they say in Rio, "You have forty-five minutes to cut your name in asphalt": which is to say, have your picture taken wearing a smashing outfit or cutting a marvelous step or displaying a fabulous body—the picture that will flash all over the vast subcontinent of Brazil or turn up a week later in a glossy issue of *Manchete* or travel by satellite or filmcan to remote, nearly unimaginable places, like Germany or Japan. Carnival is the greatest example of participatory culture yet offered to twentieth-century man. It teases the anonymous housemaid or sewing machine operator with the ancient dream of Cinderella. It raises the awesome possibility that after this one night of nights life may never again be the same for raggedy Rita or scruffy Sam. No wonder that in Rio even the poorest of the poor find their fifty cents every week to pay the price of their *fantasia*.

The Designers

The single most important man in a samba school, apart from its money-raising president, is the designer. A handful of dedicated and resourceful designers has done more to give the modern Carnival its distinctive look than have all the black masses, the officials of RioTur or the government of the state of Rio de Janeiro. Though some of these men make substantial sums today for their work, their involvement in the Carnival, which dates back twenty years in some cases, is just as selfless and idealistic as that of any member of the school. Nor should one underestimate the amount of grief involved in working with people like the *sambistas*, who are both highly emotional and given to deeds of desperate violence. Designing for a samba school is a very exacting calling and the penalty for failure can be high.

The greatest of all the Carnival designers is Fernando Pamplona, a good-looking, animated, and rather professorial man in his late forties, who responded to my request for an interview by reserving a table at a tiny and very quiet restaurant, where he insisted on ordering up an excellent meal for me and my party. During the course of our dinner, he offered a brilliant nonstop lecture that ranged over the history and character of the Carnival to which he has dedicated his life. Pamplona is nominally a scene designer, but actually he should be classified as a *regisseur:* a master theatrician who conceives and designs a great spectacle, takes executive control over every aspect of its mounting, and finally is discovered on opening night, as was once George Balanchine, seated at a sewing machine putting the final touches on a dancer's brassiere.

Like any true Carnival enthusiast, Pamplona has devoted most of his creative life to the service of a single school: Salgueiro. He first became prominent in the school in the mid-sixties, at the time when the pageants were finally coming under the discipline of art and design. He conceived and executed about a decade's worth of pageants for the school, building it up to the most exciting presence on the boulevards. He exploited brilliantly the school's innate theatrical flair by inventing countless devices for dramatizing its themes with Afro textiles, totem sculptures, shaggy fetishes, scampering animals, and ranks upon ranks of Zulus, Ibos, and Bantus, wearing masks, carrying spears, charging down the avenue in a series of brilliant bursts of theatrical color that carried all before them. Working with two assistants who eventually became important figures in their own right—the costume designer, Arlindo Rodriguez, and the scenographer, Joãzinho Trinta—Pamplona created single-handedly the whole modern rhetoric of the ethnically oriented Carnival show. He was particularly resourceful in extending the rather limited equipment of the parades by adding a lot of props, effigies, and symbols to the dancers' outfits. He was the first to exploit the space over the marchers' heads, filling it with banners, signs, and objects held up on poles: a new vertical dimension demanded by the fact that the performers were being viewed from stands stepping ever higher in air that made the human figure seem small and remote.

Pamplona's innovations cost something, to be sure. Once the dancers have been massed and fitted out with hand props like Roman legionnaires in a Hollywood movie or like extras in the second act of *Aida*, they become a show-biz phalanx that can be thrown at the audience with tremendous effect, but they cannot do anything beyond achieving this simple visual coup. To Carnival purists this choreographing of the parades is an anathema because it makes what was traditionally an unorganized street revel with every man doing his thing into a Las Vegas spectacle. The issue is still a sensitive one in Rio. Like every artistic innovation in history, the patterning of the parades demanded a price, both from the participants, who had to sacrifice some of their personal spontaneity, and from the audience, which was required to exchange its traditional expectations for a new set of values.

Pamplona's career illustrates not only the triumph of the designer over the anarchy of the Old Carnival, but also the dangers of failure for the man who assumes total responsiblity for the success of the samba school. The story of his downfall at Salgueiro has been variously reported; what it comes down to is the fact that some years ago the school suffered an exasperating defeat owing to the failure of its sound equipment. Such failures are commonplace and they have afflicted most of the schools at one time or an-

other. Portela was wiped out one year when someone came up with the brilliant idea of supplying each of the *alas* with a portable radio that could keep them in touch with the sound of their *bateria*. Thanks to the magic of radio, everybody would be able to perform in perfect harmony, instead of the forward units losing touch with the band far behind them and then executing their maneuvers out of synch with the formations in the rear.

During the long wait before the parade commenced, however, each of the radio holders removed the tape that held the tuning knob on the correct station and began exploring the dial in search of good music. When the time came to get out on the avenue and samba, most of the *alas* were unable to get back on the correct frequency. The resulting confusion destroyed the school's performance and drove Natal to the point of murder.

Something of the same sort happened the year that Pamplona got into trouble with Salgueiro; and in the wake of the fiasco, the *sambistas* began vowing vengeance on their erstwhile hero. Pamplona had devoted years of selfless labor to the school; he was not the type to throw up his hands and say, "A plague on you!" He went to a big meeting of the school's general assembly and defended himself vigorously. If he had broken down and cried, *"mea culpa!"* he would probably have been forgiven. Instead, he fought back, with the result that late at night he had to be rushed out a back door under the guard of armed friends and whisked out of the neighborhood in a fast car lest the *sambistas* catch him and kill him. After his hasty departure, his enemies held a mock execution and funeral, carrying his effigy in a coffin around the grounds of the school.

 The Pageants Explained

As nothing is more important to the modern Carnival than the Carnival pageants and as these vast parades are designed in a manner that is unintelligible to the foreign visitor, who assumes that they are merely colorful jumbles of costumed revelers instead of comprehending that they are carefully fashioned specimens of an art that flourished in Elizabethan England and Renaissance Italy, it is vital that the reader examine in some detail at least one fine example of this curious and archaic entertainment—the allegorical procession. One of the most brilliant pageants of modern times was the winner of the 1976 competition. The name of the victorious samba school, Beija-Flor ("kiss-flower" or hummingbird) was unfamiliar to most of the spectators because this club was a relative newcomer, having appeared in Class I competition only twice before and being based in a town that lies outside of Rio: Nilopolis, a poor dingy place, about an hour's drive from the city, a town which serves principally as a dormitory for the thousands of maids and workers who come into Rio every day on the railroad. Nobody expected Beija-Flor to win, least of all its own directors, who hoped at most to lay the foundation with this year's presentation for an eventual victory the following year. The school's greatest strength—apart from the enthusiasm of its members and the wealth of its presiding family, Syrian or Jewish *bicheiros*—was its new creative director, the most inspired and original Carnival designer of the present day, João Trinta.

A tiny, vivacious man with the kinky hair of the Negro, the tan skin color of a Portuguese, and the eyes of an Oriental or an Indian, João Trinta, known as Joãozinho because of his diminutive stature, was no newcomer to the boulevards. He had been the third member of the finest design team in Rio during the years when Fernando Pamplona and Arlindo Rodriguez had guided the triumphant fortunes of the most theatrical of the samba schools, Salgueiro (the red and white). When Pamplona and Rodriguez left the school, Trinta stepped into their place and proved his genius immediately by designing and mounting the prize-winning pageants for two years running. Had he remained with Salgueiro, it was widely believed that he would have made the school a three-time champion, an honor that had been achieved by three of the Big Four—Mangueira, Portela, and Imperio Serrano—but never by the Salgueiro. Instead, he elected to break with Salgueiro for reasons that are too delicate to publish but which had a lot to do with the school's financial problems. In stepping down from the Big Four, he took his creative life in his hands. But he knew exactly what he was doing, and his collaboration with the school from Nilopolis proved that both designer and school were made for each other.

Trinta's first idea for Beija-Flor was, simply as an idea, a winner. Instead of offering yet another yawning ode to Brazil or Bahia or Africa, instead of flooding the avenue for the hundredth time with Afro textiles and Indian feathers, instead of researching obscure cults and tedious legends, instead of the remote, the exotic, the patriotic, and the trite, he offered a theme that was close as the corner, familiar as the palm of your hand, yet utterly original and virtually risqué: nothing less than Rio's favorite game and the golden fount from which Carnival flows—the *jogo do bicho*!

It was a brilliant idea, an idea whose time had come. The Game was not only basic to Rio and Carnival: it was fraught with delightful visual and plastic imagery. What made the idea irresistible, however, was the fact that it could be associated with a final tribute to the King of the Game, the legendary Natal, who had died the previous April. For half a century, Natal had watched over the fortunes of his club, seeing it grow from a rabble of knife- and razor-toting hoodlums into the pomp of a great national institution. Now he was dead and the strict rules of Carnival forbade his own school from offering him homage in its annual pageant. There was nothing in the rules, however, that forbade another school from making the longed-for gesture. It even had a sort of family appropriateness because Portela is Beija-Flor's *compadre* and the two schools bear the same blue and white colors.

The *samba enredo* proved to be a good serviceable piece of work: It evoked the origins of the *jogo do bicho* and then turned to pay handsome tribute to Natal in a classic apostrophe, such as a Roman laureate might have composed for a dead Caesar or a French poet for a deceased Louis. The music rattled through a sequence of trite but singable passages. The groundwork was adequate, but the whole art of the thing lay in the hands of the designer who would have to inflect these conventional phrases into a brilliant work of street theater. Before describing the pageant Trinta created, let us run our eyes over his text.

The title of the poem is *Dream of a King—Play the Lion*. The allusion is to the universally held folk belief that dreams are prophetic: in this case, prophetic of which animal will turn up next day as winner of the Game. Like one of those "dream books" sold in the slums, the poem translates each dream image into a good bet: If you dream of the king, it says, play the lion; if you dream of an angel, play the butterfly, etc. The second theme is the history of the Game, which grew out of the practice of a certain Baron de Drummond, who established a lottery at his private zoo in the late nineteenth century to improve business. The final portion of the poem is a cluster of symbols and allusions designed to evoke and exalt Natal, allusions that are obscure to the foreigner but immediately comprehensible to any lower-class Carioca. The text follows with a couple of professorial notes.

Dream of a King—Play the Lion

Dream of an angel—play the butterfly,
Don't think twice about it.
Dream of a king—play the lion.
But in this festival of royal value,
Make no mistake—
Your best bet is Beija-Flor.
Singing and remembering in colors,
My dear Rio, the flower games,[1]
When the Baron de Drummond created
A garden full of animals. Hence
He created a popular lottery by
Which you could win 20,000 royals with 10 farthings.
The people began to imagine things,
Seeking under the lovely spell of dreams
Inspiration for a winner some day.

Dream of children—play the rabbit.
Dream of a stubborn person—play the donkey.
Dream of a dolled-up boy—the interpretation
Is the peacock or the deer.

---

[1] Drummond got the idea of holding a lottery at his zoo from the practice of certain florists who would reward each customer with free flowers.

With this game controlled Madueira[2]
Natal, the good Natal, who consecrated
His school to the tradition of Carnival.
His soul today is a white eagle[3]
Enfolded with a blue veil.

His Majesty, the Samba,
And His court of vagabonds,
Salute Natal in the sky.

About a week after Trinta and his school had been acclaimed winners of the samba parade, I interviewed him at the opera house, where he works as a scene designer, and sought his rationales for everything he had wrought. Sitting on a straight-backed chair in an office behind the fly gallery that was so old, bare, and desiccated that it might have been the inner chamber of a pyramid, the boyish designer alternately sang the victorious samba and explained phrase by phrase how he had embodied its meaning.

The first decision he had to make was how to open the parade. Instead of the currently popular gimmick of sticking out a line of spangled and *tanga*ed go-go girls in front of the title float (a cheap shot in a medium where there are so many legitimate opportunities to exploit "tits and ass"), Trinta opened his pageant with the traditional appearance of the *comissão de frente* ("front commission"), the minor officials of the school. He dressed these "creoles," as he calls them, in marvelous coachman's costumes, with capes and standing collars and stove-pipe hats that made them stand about seven feet tall. Then, he delivered with the *abre-alas* ("wings opener") or title float the first of several visual volleys that had the spectators shouting with glee the moment they spied the school.

On a big mechanically elaborate carnival car, he rigged two dazzling silver wheels that revolved slowly, flashing from their vaned op-art surfaces glinting reflections of all the lights along the avenue. Standing before these wheels on a revolving stage were the figures who symbolized the first line of the samba: "Dream of an angel—play the butterfly." The prettiest girls in the school, posed like Ziegfeld girls, were atop the stage in front of the glittering wheels, wearing butterfly headdresses and flaunting bodies flashing with oil and silver dust. High above them stood the angel, who turned out to be the school's most celebrated *destaque*, the pop music star, Maria Alcina.

As the poem turned next to the origins of the Game in the Baron Drummond's zoo, another huge float came rolling by: this one an evocation of the zoological garden filled with marvelous fairytale effigies of the twenty-five animals that comprise the *jogo*

---

[2] working-class district

[3] The eagle is the second number in the game and the symbol of Portela: hence, Natal's number. It was taken out of play on the day of his funeral.

do bicho—the ostrich, eagle, donkey, butterfly, dog, goat, sheep, camel, snake, rabbit, horse, elephant, rooster, cat, alligator, lion, monkey, pig, peacock, turkey, boar, tiger, bear, deer, cow.

The next float projected the essence of the samba with such strength and humor that its appearance practically provoked a demonstration. After a whole night—no, many nights for many years!—of giant totems and lumbering caravels and chunks of the Brazilian landscape, down the principal avenue of Rio came a colossal float that represented a bed on which reposed two immense Negroes, a man and his wife, each sound asleep, with the bed clothes in disarray and their huge feet with splayed toes thrusting out from beneath the sheets. Above their heads floated the whole menagerie of the animals named in the samba, with the lion's share of the space being devoted to the lion that appears in the samba's title. A shower of gold coins—the "20,000 royals"— was falling on the dreaming blacks.

The impudence, the honesty, the straight-to-the-heart effect of this marvelous evocation of Rio's black masses and their eternal dream of a hit on the animals was something that had never been seen before in Carnival but which was destined to spawn a whole generation of imitations. When I interviewed Trinta, I tried to get him to admit that there was something slyly subversive about this image, something that undercut all the pompous pretentiousness of Carnival and set it back down on the jolly ground of grotesquerie and comedy from which it had once sprung in this city. He would admit nothing of the kind, insisting only that the theme and its treatment were simply true to life in the slums, which is precisely what made the float so startling and so delectable.

There were a number of in-jokes in the parade which would not have been obvious to a foreigner. The verse that speaks of a dressed-up boy suggests a homosexual, and as every school has one or more wings of homosexuals—who are greeted the moment they appear on the streets with shouts of *bicha! bicha!* (fag! fag!)— Trinta had put these boys into the costumes of deers and peacocks. Likewise, the dream of children was represented by the wing of children. The dream of stubborn people prompted a private jest. Beija-Flor, like many modern schools, has a wing of choreographers. As a traditionalist, Trinta dislikes these people who presume to teach the *sambistas* how to dance. He expressed his opinion of their wrongheadedness by costuming them as donkeys.

The conclusion of the samba contains the line "His Majesty, the Samba, and his court of vagabonds." This verse was lifted from the very first samba in which Portela paraded with allegories. It was part of the dense clump of symbols and allusions that tied together the symbol of the school (the eagle) and its colors (blue and white), Natal's name and his number in the *jogo do bicho*, and the name of the district (Madureira) from which he and his school had come for so many years to compete and often to triumph. The conventional way to pay tribute to the great man would have been to trundle by a heroic bust of him heaped high with flowers. Trinta decided instead to employ the great white eagle, which had served so often as Portela's title float, with its solemnly beating wings.

Public Rehearsals

Traditionally, the Carnival season commences on New Year's Eve, called at Rio *Grito de Carnaval*, or "First Whoop of Carnival." According to popular humor, the first sign of the imminent Carnival is the sight of a black man chasing a stray cat: Cat skin being the finest material in the world for that curious instrument the *cuica*. Actually, Carnival comes first to public notice in November, when each school chooses its samba and prepares to "defend" it on the boulevards. From this time forth, the public begins to drift in ever-increasing numbers toward the rehearsal grounds of the schools to observe and to participate in the festive preparations for the great event. This attendance by a large and paying public at the schools' rehearsals is a sign of how socially acceptable have become the once disreputable *sambistas*. Nothing is more fashionable today than taking the long nocturnal jaunt out to the industrial slums to drink, dance and party with the *escolas*.

In the old days, a school's *terreiro*, or rehearsal ground, would have been nothing to boast about: a flat spot on a hill or, at most, a local *quadro*, a small indoor soccer arena. Today, stacked up the hill of Mangueira there is still the same old huddle of deplorable squatters' shacks; but planted smack in their midst, looming above them like a cathedral in a Brooklyn slum, is a big cast-concrete samba stadium. Blazing in the night with banks of powerful floodlights mounted on steel towers, the *terreiro* looks from a distance like an American ballpark.

"Rehearsal" (*ensãio*) in this case is just a euphemism for a fund-raising party. In fact, the practice of charging admission and taking a cut on all the food and drink served in the course of an all-night rave-up makes the schools' public rehearsals exact analogues of that ancient institution of the black American slums —the rent party. The schools have a lot more to pay for than the rent, so the more commercially resourceful *escolas* have adopted the practice of holding rehearsals not only on their home turf but at public arenas much closer to the prosperous residents and tourists of the Southern Zone. Portela, for example, holds rehearsals every Friday, Saturday, and Sunday night during the entire month preceding Carnival. The rehearsals are held at three locations every night: a total of twenty-seven rehearsals every weekend. Averaging about $7,000 a rehearsal, the school earns about $250,000 during that month. The school will spend close to a million dollars on Carnival.

One serious objection can be made to the rehearsals: They have become so popular and so crassly commercial that they offer nothing to the genuine samba lover. The real rehearsals at which the various *alas* perfect their choreography are kept secret, lest a rival school steal the steps. The full-scale rehearsals during which the school marshals its entire company and puts it through the pageant it will perform on the avenue are conducted on weekend afternoons in the streets of the schools' home districts, which are roped off by police for this purpose. To see good, authentic samba dancing by nimble and resourceful performers, therefore, you have to get away from the mobs at the big rehearsals and go out to the *quadros* in the remote industrial districts where the little schools hold their *ensãios*, drawing a predominantly local crowd who come just for the dancing. These *quadros* are an hour's drive from Copacabana along a maze of ill-marked and feebly illuminated freeways, avenues, and streets.

The journey to the lower-class districts is an eye-opener. It shows the reverse side of Copacabana and Ipanema. Instead of miles of gleaming new apartment houses and bustling commercial avenues, you rush past garishly colored stucco facades from the last century, block after block of dingy little houses flush with the street, and commercial areas that have the glaring squalid look of Harlem at night. Rio is not a city of prosperous, white, upper- or middle-class men and women who spend their days loafing at the beach. This obvious fact is often overlooked by the tourist who spends his entire visit caught in the silken net of the *Zona Sul*. Rio is dirty cement, scabrous brick, broken sidewalks, rasping old buses, and tens of thousands of people who never wear shoes. It is these people who created the samba and its culture. It is they who are the real *sambistas*. It is with them that you should spend at least a part of the Carnival.

When you walk into a typical *quadro*, you feel like you've stepped onto a set for *West Side Story*. There will be tough-looking dudes lounging at the gate, quaint macho practices like free admissions for the ladies. Inside you will find a bar and tables, a large clear space for dancing, and at one end a *bateria*, or percussion band, and a singer: essentially the same arrangements that you find in a big samba stadium. What will be totally different is the atmosphere. There will be no crowds of strangers, no commotion on the floor, no harangues over the public address system, as the officials of the school struggle to maintain order. Instead, you'll get the true flavor of a working class social club filled with very relaxed and friendly people. There will be lots of table-hopping, conversation between friends and acquaintances, affectionate embraces, and a few old drunks staggering around, sometimes cutting comic steps. An official of the school may invite you to his table and offer you a *batido*: heavily sweetened, luridly colored fruit juice laced with *cachaça* or bootleg rum. You may even receive a spontaneous salute by one of the school's *porta-bandeiras*, or banner-bearers, twirling the flag before you. Whatever happens, you can be sure that you will see some brilliant and joyous dancing and hear some powerful percussion music.

The *bateria* is the heart and soul of a samba school. When it

plays for a street parade, it may sound powerful, pungent, or even awesome—but it rarely sounds interesting. Only when it settles down at a rehearsal like this to play through the night does it reveal everything it knows how to do. In this age of remorseless rhythm, when the effects of sitting for hours drinking, smoking dope, and listening to beat music are so well known, it might be asked, "What does one get from listening to such a primitive band?" The answer can be summed up in one word: *Africa*. The night-long elaboration of endless designs in percussion is the whole art of African music: an art with which only a few travelers and musicologists have made acquaintance. A fascinating and difficult art, African drumming has an especially great appeal for Americans, brought up as they are on black rhythms and jazz, which last can be seen as a sublimation of the vocal half of African music into an instrumental idiom.

All night long the samba school's band plays the same basic rhythm at the same tempo. They have no melody instruments, no harmony, frequently no vocal line. Their music is percussion per se. Yet on top of the basic beat, they superimpose such an astounding variety of counter-rhythms, solo assertions, and other musical events that the effect—far from being monotonous or hypnotic—is fascinating, electrifying, and finally, stunning. When you leave the rehearsal, the drums resound in your mind for hours.

The most remarkable single feature of the drumming of the *baterias* is the riveting-gun solos of the *tamborims*. Like so many of the instruments employed in Carnival, these little hand drums have no direct counterpart in the instrumentarium of the Western world. A *tamborim* is not a tambourine but a small one-headed drum about the size of an embroidery hoop. It is held firmly in one hand and struck by the other hand with a split stick of wood or steel about sixteen inches in length. A practiced player can make this tiny instrument cut through even the largest percussion band in precisely the way a pistol shot cuts through the sound of a mob. The sound is so sharp and explosive, the sequence of such sounds so arresting, that even after hours of listening, one is still startled by every such outburst.

The other instrument that attracts special attention is the *cuica*. This is another one-headed drum about the size of a four-quart pot. A thin stick embedded in the head of the drum hangs down inside the center of the instrument. The player holds this stick with a bit of sponge or rag dipped in resin and rubs it up and down, imparting grating vibrations to the drum head. The sound that emerges varies from grunting to braying to bleating. What it most resembles is the cry of the little jungle mammal for which the instrument is named: the *cuica*. By pressing on the drum head with his other hand, the player can modify the pitch and timbre of the sound, making it bleat up high or grumble down low. The direction of the sound is focused by affixing to the more elaborate instruments a couple of curved horns, like old-fashioned hearing aids or speaking trumpets, which project from the forward edge.

The equivalent in the percussive street band of the string bass in the jazz band, the *cuica* is the timekeeper, the tempo holder, the rhythmic anchor around which the other instruments execute their maneuvers. The best *cuicenists* are extremely agile and dextrous; they can make the instrument race along at fast tempos or execute hiccuplike intervals or even play elementary tunes. (One of the saddest features of street virtuosity is that so often it is an attempt to torture a rudimentary device into the kind of performance that could be elicited easily from a more sophisticated instrument. Virtuosity in the slums is often just a matter of doing things the hard way—which is the only way open to such desperately deprived but genuinely talented and expressive folk.)

The most awesome instrument of the battery is the bass tom-tom, which is called the *surdo* or "deaf man." This drum is struck with a solid wooden mallet and damped the next instant by the player's left hand so as to produce a deep, resonant but sharply defined thump. The *surdo* is a descendant of the hollow logs employed in the so-called jungle telegraph.

The tribal atmosphere—not of war but of peace and play—is strong during the rehearsal. People of every age and description will get out on the floor and shake it up. Everything goes at once because the *sambista* is an individualist. When he dances he does his own thing without the slightest concern for what the others are doing.

The first thing to grasp about samba dancing is its basic simplicity. It's called a dance but it's more like a strut; a jive-assed nigger street strut, sassy and sexy—really nothing more than a hip way of getting across town. When you see the *sambistas* out in the street or at a ball, they always have their arms raised and open, with the wrist bent in like a ballerina. This is a gracious, exultant, and classic gesture that frames the head, the face, the smile, and the provocative eye: a gesture suggestive of joy, and openness, of the woman's embrace of the man's body in grateful pleasure. When you look at the dancers' feet, all they are doing is a loose-kneed shuffle, with their soles scraping the ground and their hips pushing forward rhythmically or rocking from side to side. This basic pattern is well suited to the street or the ballroom where there is no space to really shake a leg. It represents the samba in its minimal form, as the suggestion of a dance.

When the *sambistas* are released into open space, they suddenly become real dancers. They lower their arms and concentrate on their feet. Instead of shuffling along at half time, they pick up the fast beat and swing into variation one. This is that heel-and-toe, one-foot-behind-the-other step that suggests so strongly the Charleston. Once a female dancer starts flying with this step, her ass swings like crazy. This released ass is what you concentrate upon as you go into variation two, which is the customary break and breather from the fast step. Now the dancer comes back to half time, but she bumps and grinds her pudenda hard as she shuffles across the floor with the legs well apart, producing jelly tremors up and down her thighs that make the men go wild. She is the ideal realization of that classic American blues verse: "Wanna big woman, meat shakin' on the bones."

If the *sambista* has a partner, some sharp dude who has really got his act together, he will take off into double time doing the same step as she; then, he'll go into the acrobatic steps that are the special province of the *mestre sala*, or major domo. He'll bend forward until he looks like he's doing a buck-and-wing, with his head down to the floor; or he'll throw his head back and kick up his heels like he's doing the cakewalk. He may suddenly do a *tour jeté* or a leg-lock that threatens to topple him to the floor or a hesitation step that stops him in mid-stride like a strobe light. When the break comes, he'll leap into the air and come down on his knees. Leaning way back, with his head just a couple feet above the floor, he'll extend his arms and wiggle his fingers, making a beckoning gesture toward his partner, as if to say: "Sock it to me, baby!" Then the woman will advance with her pussy pumping and her ass wiggling furiously, in a parody of lust. When she works her way to where her partner is kneeling, the woman will straddle his body and slowly squat on his face, never abandoning the pumping motion. When she's down so far she's practically sitting on him, he jackknifes up and ducks nimbly between her legs, making his escape. In another version of this same variation, the two partners squat down together, bumping back and forth, with the woman astride the man's thigh. As they lower their torsos, they hold out their arms and do that Hindu neck motion that was called back in the days of that forgotten dance, the shorty George, "peckin'."

Another style of dancing the samba is what Brazilians call *gafieira*, or "honky-tonk." The dancers hold each other closely but off center so that as they spin about they use their bodies as counterweights. The legs are kept tightly together and the steps are very small as the partners move around the floor switching from side to side. After the first steps, in which the partners merely alternate sides, the man may pick up the woman and bounce her rhythmically from one thigh to the other. (The same step was employed in the "aerial" lindy of the forties.) After the bounces, the partners straighten up and go back to their tight face-off positions, braking to sudden stops and back bends or doing tight twirls that suggest the movements of a toreador performing his veronicas. This style has archaic elements, like bows and handkerchief steps. It is performed in special clubs that are called *gafieiras*.

I've never seen the end of a samba *ensãio*. The parties never break up until dawn. You have to be Brazilian to maintain the full pace of Carnival. Or you have to be crazy!

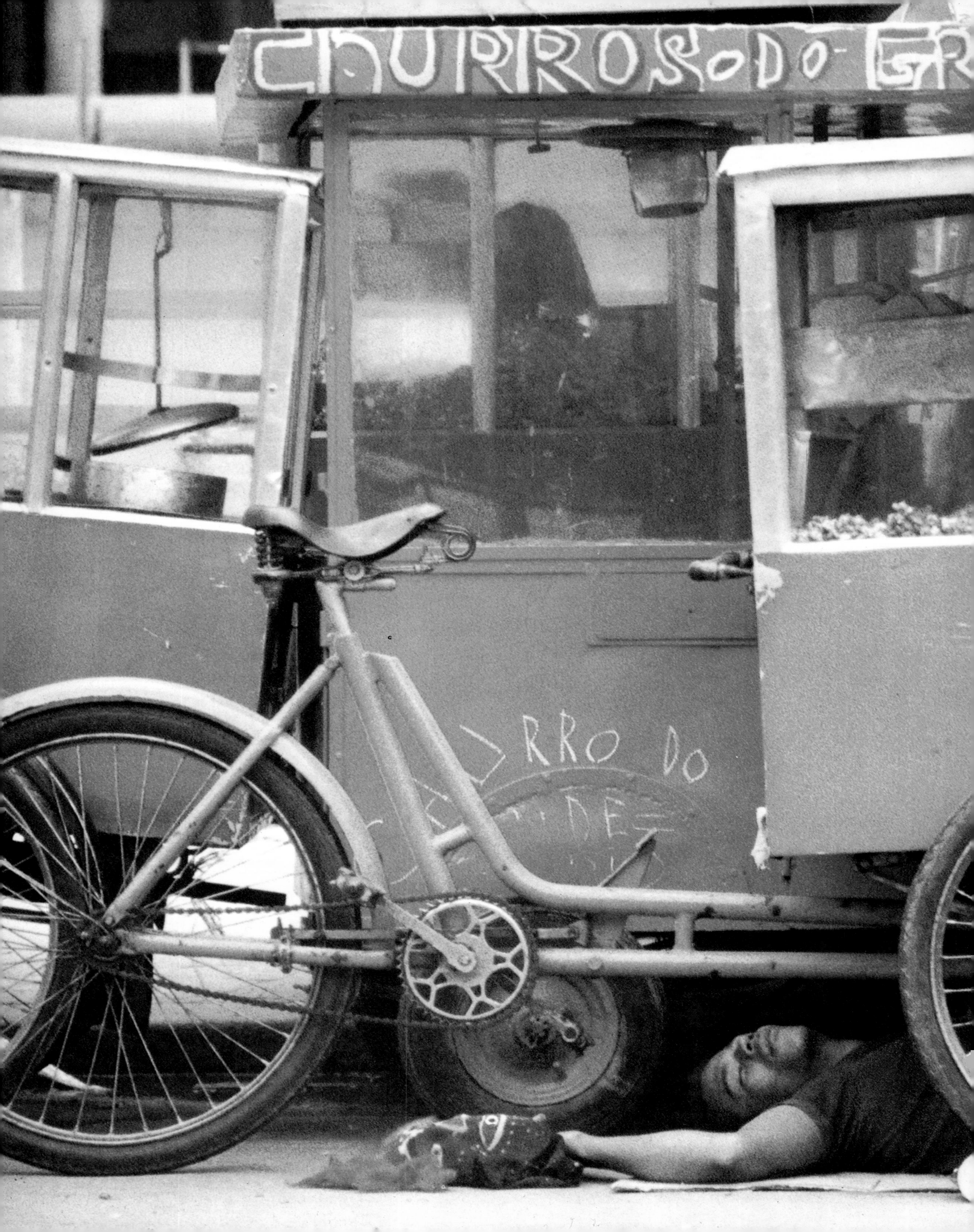
CHURROS DO GR

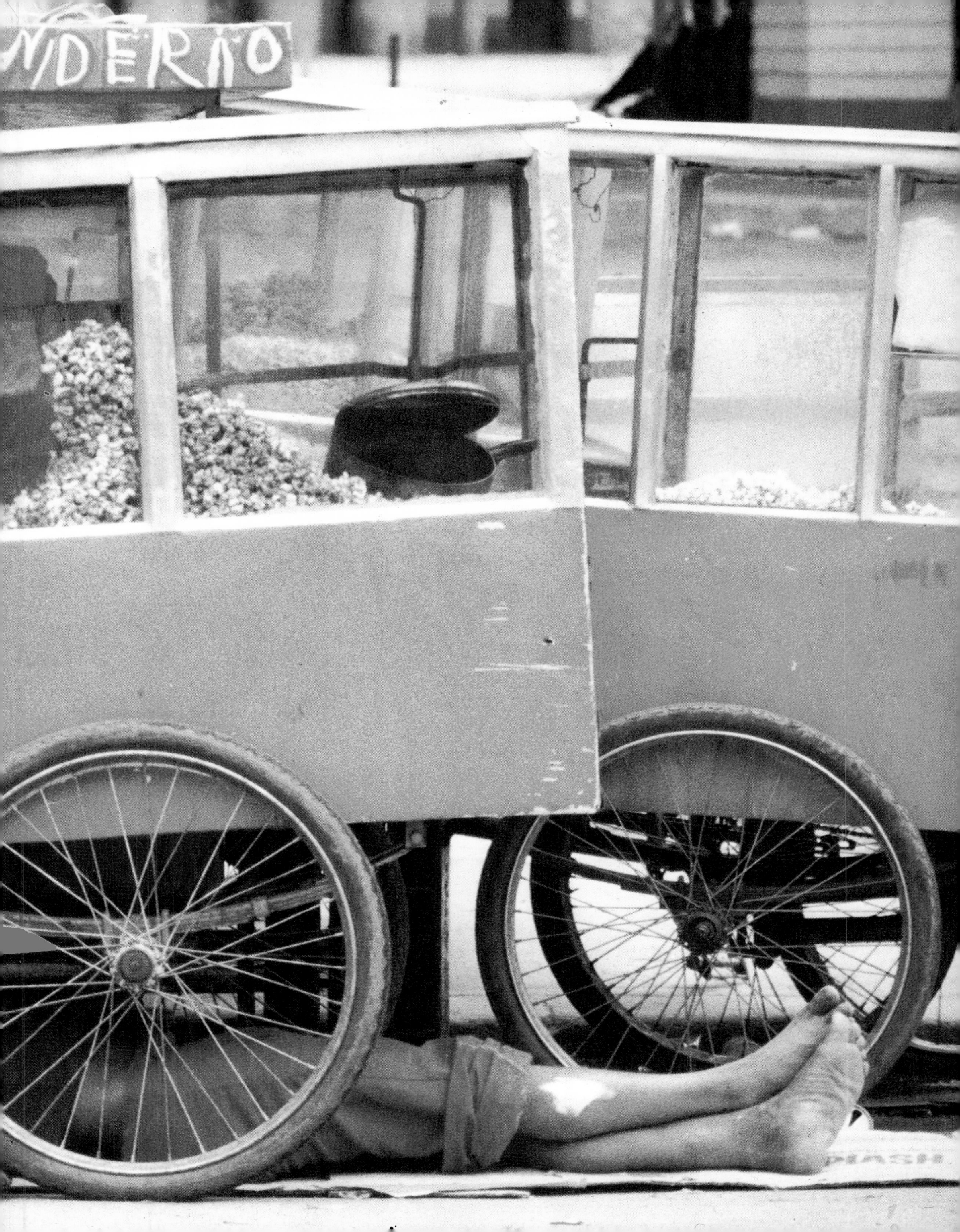
NDERIO

The Old Carnival

While the tourists sun themselves on the beaches of Copacabana and Ipanema, while the poor blacks party through the night in the industrial slums of the north, most of Rio's middle class flees the city. The heat, the swarming hordes of visitors, the interruption of normal services, and the hubbub of Carnival are the reasons why most people who can afford to leave the city on this great national holiday take off for the cool and lovely mountains to the west or the remote beaches to the north or south. As for those who remain, they join the tourists on the sands of the city beaches or hang out at certain favored cafes where they sing, laugh, drink, shout, and jump to the music of old-fashioned bands that belt out a boozy, beery, trombonish sort of music such as you might imagine having been played at the Moulin Rouge.

As for the possibility of really getting involved in Carnival, the vast majority of the middle class dismisses the thought out of hand. Indeed, one of the most surprising discoveries that a foreigner makes in Rio at Carnival season is that everyone, from illiterate hack drivers to sophisticated intellectuals, believes that Carnival is dead. They will tell you that Carnival, once, was a wondrous thing, a festival of all the people, a spontaneous revel, a mass take-off into regions of fun and innocent delight. They will say that today's Carnival is an industry, a Las Vegas show put on for tourists or a government trick to dissipate the revolutionary impulses of the people. Certainly, forty years ago, Carnival was another thing belonging to another age, another class, another Rio.

Instead of the violent, noisy, insufferable concrete jungle that is Rio today, the city of the 1930s was quiet and harmonious, filled with fine old baroque and Victorian buildings. Instead of the fuming crush of hundreds of hulking buses and snarling motor cars, the public transport consisted of old-fashioned open trolley cars, like the ones that still wind up to Santa Teresa. The population, too, was different from the present-day Cariocas. Instead of the racial ragout that is modern Rio, the central city was predominantly white and middle class. The women wore the long, tight skirts of the thirties and big, sweeping picture hats. Men presented an even more startling contrast to today's Cariocas. Instead of wearing short-sleeved, floral-patterned shirts, whose tails hang out, those gentlemen of a not-so-distant past were fully dressed, even at the height of summer, in white suits, Panama hats and neatly tied cravats. The ideal Brazilian male of that era was bone-thin, diminutive in stature, with patent-leather hair, large luminous eyes, prominent cheek bones, thin lips, aquiline nose, a pencil-line moustache, and, in older men, deeply graven lines down the cheeks.

Carnival was then essentially a masquerade. Everyone donned his *fantasia* and mask and went about in the streets asking, "Do you know me?" It was Halloween for adults. Harlequins and Pierrots, pirates and devils were everywhere interspersed with picturesque figures from the Hollywood screen. Chaplin with his waddle and spinning cane; Tom Mix in stetson and chaps, twirling his lariat; Valentino in gaucho outfit, little pom-poms jiggling on the brim of his sombrero; the bohemian girl with her fancy gypsy skirts and bangles; the Chinaman; the hula-skirted Hawaiian; the American Indian; and all the other exotics that Hollywood had domesticated. The most interesting *fantasias*, however, were those that were purely Carioca: the man costumed as a big old-fashioned box camera or the elegantly ruffled and pantalooned clown carrying a sign reading (in Portuguese): "Bloco— I Am Alone."

The daytime Carnival of those years was dominated by one great event: the *corso*, or parade of motor cars, which began far out at the limits of the city in the then distant beach resort of Copacabana (accessible only by a single two-lane road) and proceeded into the city through Botafogo, Flamengo, Catete, Gloria, Lapa, until it rolled in triumph down the city's principal boulevard, the Avenida Rio Branco. In those days the Rio Branco was not the roaring, stinking, exhaust-beclouded traffic sewer that it is today. It was a magnificent European boulevard, broad, tree shaded, lined on either side with handsome baroque buildings in French empire style: big massive stone structures with florid carving, fancy wrought-iron work, flamboyant domes, and the flying roof statuary beloved of Iberian architects.

In those days the possession of an automobile was a sign of wealth and status. Car designs were still suggestive of the elegant barouches, phaetons, and broughams of the nineteenth century. Long touring cars could let down their canvas tops so that beautifully costumed revelers could stand upright on the seats and running boards to wave their arms, blow kisses, toss confetti and serpentines, or reach forward with a roguish look to squirt perfumed ether in the spectators' open faces. By the time the cars reached the Rio Branco, they had been bombarded with so many brightly colored streamers that they trailed yards of thickly twined paper which linked one car to another in an endless chain that extended from the center of the city to its outermost suburbs and back again.

While the *corso* was crawling in and out of the city, there was much merrymaking on the beaches. There were mock battles between *blocos* of Indians and conquistadors. Couples in bathing suits fox-trotted, and historic events were enacted by *carnavalescos*, like those who landed from a ship in Guanabara Bay impersonating Pedro Alvarez Cabral taking possession of the country in the sixteenth century. Probably the most charming custom was the dawn dip after an all-night ball. Dancers would rush to the beach as the blood-red sunrise came crepitating across the waves. Wearing bathing suits under their paper costumes, they would let their wet *fantasias* float free, emerging from the sea purged of Carnival.

Even in those days of feeble artificial lighting, the most fascinating spectacles were those that took place by night. The richly costumed *ranchos* (middle-class social clubs) would march with their bands playing grandly melancholic *marchas*. The Great Societies (society clubs), then at the peak of their power, would astound the populace with the grandeur of their huge and costly *alegorias* (lit. "allegories" or floats). Unlike the floats of today, which must be pushed by hand, the Great Societies paraded with massive constructions that could reach a length of one hundred and fifty feet. Elaborately sculpted and painted, these immense floats were sometimes heroic in style, sometimes grotesque, sometimes realistic, sometimes surrealistic. There might be a grouping of grandiose national figures in that epic style so popular with the Nazis and the designers of the Rockefeller Center. Or the float might carry a colossal figure of Rex Carnaval or some grotesque creature of Brazilian folklore. The finest floats had moving parts: banks of oars stroking rhythmically along the sides of a great galley, or Art Deco buildings flanked by a solemnly swinging crane. Emblazoned with the names of the famous nineteenth-century societies—Os Tenentes do Diablo ("Lieutenants of the Devil"), Os Democraticos ("The Democratics"), Os Fenianos ("The Fenians")—the *alegorias* were freighted with dozens of pretty girls, blowing thousands of kisses or tossing flowers from baskets into the crowds. They moved very slowly, with great pomp, drawn by long teams of plumed and caparisoned horses.

What made the spectacle sublime was the awesome illumination afforded by Bengal lights, torches filled with incandescent powders that burned in various colors, giving off a lurid glare and great whiffs of acrid smoke. What a spectacle they must have made as they moved to the solemn processional beat of the drums, the yearning, straining melodies of the brass and strings, with the voices of the marchers crying aloud the poetry of Carnival to the night air, while great crowds of spectators gazed with fascination on the immense allegoric shapes floating past in the fitful and fantastic light of the colored torches. Thus did the old Carnival proceed through the heart of Rio like a great religious pageant or ecclesiastical cortege.

Now that the beautiful old Rio of the thirties has fallen victim to the wrecker's ball and the enchanting and innocent Carnival of that era has been driven off the boulevards by the jungle drums of the Third World's *Masse Mensch* is it any wonder that most white Cariocas and most older people of all races should regard the loss of the old Carnival with keen nostalgia and regret?

The Beautiful People Arrive

The Beautiful People arrive at Rio about a week before Carnival. In their Mark Cross wallets and Louis Vuitton bags are stuffed reservations to the finest hotels, tickets for balls and parades, lists of outstanding restaurants and discotheques and—most important—invitations from rich, hospitable Cariocas who make it their business to show the glamorous foreigners around Rio: at least those parts of Rio in which a Brazilianaire feels most comfortable and self-satisfied. Even the most blasé traveler is thrilled by his first visit. For the journey to Carnival is not simply a trip across time zones, continents, or cultures: It is a magical passage from winter to summer.

When you board the plane in, say, New York, the city is lying dead and gray, like a burnt-out fleet scuttled in shallow water. The dun air has the raw, damp feel of February. Bundled up like Dr. Zhivago in leather boots, lambskin-lined suede coat and fur hat, the New York Muscovite enters the cabin of the Varig airliner like Old Man Winter. After a couple of drinks and a meal served by neat little stewards, you doze fitfully through the long dark night. Early next morning, after refreshing yourself and casting a few curious glances at the carpet of thick green jungle showing through rifts in the clouds, you land outside Rio. Though it is only eight in the morning, the red sky looks like a giant electric broiler, just switched on, glowing ruddily and promising a rapid buildup of oppressive heat.

Then begins the long ride south to Copacabana. At first you run past raw industrial squalor of a kind that is hard to find in modern Europe or America. It looks like Pittsburgh forty years ago. Mills belching smoke. Ragged iron sheds. Black laborers stripped to the waist, crowned with orange hard hats. The traffic that you run with and often stall behind is also of a kind that antedates the modern concern with air pollution and environmental protection. Black nauseating fumes fart from the tailpipes of tough-looking Mercedes buses. Dozens of little Volkswagen bugs go skittering before you, like a race of brightly colored cockroaches.

These satanic mills comprise the world of Rio's industrial slaves. It is a world that for all its poverty, ugliness, and horror has produced the lifeblood of Brazilian culture. The industrial and commercial districts through which you are passing—Ramos, Bonsucceso, and later, Tijuca—are samba country. If you were to turn right off this highway and penetrate the maze of roads and streets that lies in that direction, you would come in time to Meier, Cavalcanti, Cascadura, Oswaldo Cruz, and Madureira, the last the heartland of the samba. Driving for half an hour through densely congested traffic, you finally reach the heart of the city and go sweeping along the ancient dockside. You catch a distant glimpse of stony nineteenth-century buildings, lush trees, riotous Carnival decorations. Just a flash—then you're clear of the old city and racing toward the beautiful new world of the masters.

Lilting along a graceful, curving parkway, you gaze at the ranks of gleaming white modernistic buildings on one side and the pretty bay on the other side, backed by Rio's celebrated thumbs-up volcanic mountains. Now you gaze at the fleet of yachts anchored in Botafogo Bay. Suddenly, you plunge into a great tunnel through the mountains; its entire face has been decorated with a bright plastic mural of clowns and carnivalesques. Through the tunnel you hum until you pop out the other side, reaching at last the ocean beach and the classic picture-postcard prospect of Copacabana.

The French are whisked to the Meridien, a monstrous slab of brown glass framed in concrete, which stands with its shoulder to the beach at Copacabana. On the ground floor, the visitors discover an immaculate replica of the Café de la Paix, nicknamed by the local wits the "Café de la Guerre" because of the rudeness of the waiters. Below street level, they will party at the local chapter of Regine's, whose manageress, a tall, striking woman from Haiti, is the only negress one ever encounters at chic white penthouse parties.

The English and Americans are quartered down the beach at an even taller and more out-of-scale skyscraper, built by an immensely wealthy local family, the Bezerra de Mellos, and named after one of its sons, Othon, *i.e.*, Otto. The Othon Palace was not really ready for its first Carnival in 1976, but the management honored the reservations just the same. The result? An incredible fiasco. The automatic elevators failed, and the guests were compelled to climb ten or fifteen floors to their rooms. The servants had not been properly trained and organized; the beds remained unmade until three in the afternoon, with breakfast served at lunchtime. The little pool on the roof of the hotel, hopelessly inadequate in any case, was not properly connected to the filtration system. Bathing in its viscous green water was like swimming in the Ganges. After a week of failed phones, missed meals, and heart-attack hikes up service stairs, the name of the hotel had changed: it was now referred to as "The Awful Palace."

Matters prospered a little better in Rio's other new five-star hotels, but they all had their problems. The most aggressively publicized, the Naçional, is a towering glass cylinder which zooms up like a rocket ship straining for release from the beach at Barra de Tijuca, a very distant beach destined to become the next Ipanema. The first big building to be erected in what has now become a typically Brazilian jiffyville of hastily constructed high-rise apartment houses, hotels, and retail markets, the Naçional was a bold attempt to break the monopolisitic hold of Copacabana on the tourist trade. Unfortunately, the builders ran out of money before

the hotel was furnished. They were compelled to line the startlingly futuristic shell with the same furnishings and carpets that are used in American motel chains. They were also compelled to send their guests to the beach across an express highway. Nor did they solve the problem of shortening the access to the hotel from the airport—a long journey that entails circumnavigating the entire perimeter of the city.

All of Rio's hotel problems arise from the fact that until recently the city counted for nothing in the international vacation and resort business. The whole city had but two or three deluxe hotels and these were of a size more befitting the nineteenth than the twentieth century. Then one day, the generals in Brazilia decided that Rio should rival Acapulco or Miami. EmbraTur, Brazil's national travel trust, announced that it would underwrite construction costs and guarantee returns on investments. Overnight, gigantic hotels were thrown up with no staffs to operate them, no managements to direct them, and no technology to keep them running. Hence the debacles of 1976.

The sophisticated people, the rich people, the people who have been coming to Rio for years, you will rejoice to hear, were not inconvenienced in the slightest by Rio's growing pains. When they decided that they would attend Carnival, they did what they always do: They got on the phone to Rio's most fabulous hotel, one of the last remaining hotels in the modern world that still evokes the opulent atmosphere of the Grand Hotel. This hotel is a trip in itself: a time trip back to the twenties and thirties, when a hotel (a word used formerly to designate an aristocrat's urban palace) was a glamorous modern institution, a social microcosm that stimulated the imaginations of the greatest writers, such as Marcel Proust or Thomas Mann. So many movies and TV shows have been made about this hotel that it is now regarded as a national landmark. The mere mention of its name conjures up the whole dream of flying down to Rio—The Copacabana Palace.

A masterpiece of ice-cream baroque, the Copa is constantly being threatened with demolition because it spreads its low-rise bulk, with an aristocrat's disregard for the cost of the seat, over twelve thousand square meters of the most valuable land in the world. In the gleaming two-mile grin of Copacabana Beach, the Copa is the only stumpy tooth. With its ostentatiously modest entrance tucked behind an old-fashioned horseshoe driveway, and its fabulous 1920s Hollywood swimming pool occupying enough space to put up a whole new hotel, The Copa sits way back from the city's desperately crowded building line murmuring contemptuously, "Let them eat beans!"

A fortress of privilege and a citadel of contempt for modern efficiency and economy, the Copa comprises a whole colony of annexes and dependencies, apartments and theaters, nightclubs and gambling casinos, ballrooms and restaurants, bars, flower shops, and *bijouteries*. The only thing that the creators of this monstrous white elephant neglected to supply was rooms for the guests. Though the hotel is immense, the number of rooms is miniscule. All told, there are in this gigantic establishment only 150 rooms and suites. By rights, the cheapest room should be $100 a day and double that at Carnival. In fact, the rooms are priced competitively with a motel in New York. Like so many privileges enjoyed by the rich and famous, residence at the Copa is a bargain. The joke is that the bargain is not even hard to get. People appear at the last minute before Carnival—when you can't find an empty dog house in Rio—and they get a room at the Copa. Apparently, everybody is so in awe of the place and so put off by its official policy—you must have a signed, pre-paid contract for your room drawn up the preceding year—that they never give a thought to staying at the very finest place from which to sally forth to Carnival.

It is natural to be cowed by the Copa. Its aura of sublime self-involvement and self-complacency is such that you feel the management has done you great favor by allowing you to walk through the door. Instead of signing the register, you want to kiss the clerk's hand. When the old bellman escorts you down the long, imperial yellow corridor with its gleaming parquet floor and the maid bows with a smile, you want to burst into tears. It's too good to be true! Then, when you enter your high-ceilinged chamber with its quaint old tropicana furniture and the servant throws aside the drapes with a flourish and cranks up the ancient shutters, you gasp as you gaze at the beach. There it is—the post-card! The greatest beach view in all the world snapped from the most perfect angle. And it all belongs to you! If you're travelling with a woman, you have to exercise incredible discipline not to scream and jump around like Hitler when he learned that Paris had surrendered. It takes something stronger than modesty not to spin on your heel and crow, "Well, baby, whatdya think of the old boy now?"

Instead, you order a drink. Scotch and soda, *por favor*. For room service, you get a replay of a thirties' movie. The waiter, a veteran with a face like Bert Lahr, arrives with tray on shoulder and folding table in hand. A practiced snap of the wrist and the table is extended in place; a graceful descending gesture and the tray has landed on the spot. Instead of a prepoured shot and a little bottle of Canadian Club, you are offered a whole quart of costly, imported Black Label, worth about $60 in a Brazilian hotel. A strip of paper is pasted on the side of the bottle marking off the shots. An old-fashioned siphon full of hissing bubbles stands beside the bottle. If you grew up watching thirties' movies, the epiphany is awesome, the gratification beyond words. At last, you are Fred Astaire!

When you descend in the old hand-operated lift, you step through the silver screen straight into movieland. Here before you lies the original Hollywood pool, the archetype of that costly and luxurious appointment whose beauty and glamour has been pissed away in a million suburban backyards. The pool is big and green, surrounded by a broad flagstone patio shaded with tropical trees and furnished with old-fashioned, white wooden porch furniture. The guests are fleshy middle-aged matrons, bronze-headed baldies and spoiled little brats. As you marvel at the indifference these people show towards their flabby bodies and ugly bathing suits, you ponder that great mystery of the rich: how they transcend self-consciousness.

Who are these people? Well, take that deeply tanned, predatory-looking man sitting with his comrades, laughing and drinking at a poolside table. He is Prince von Thurn und Taxis, one of the wealthiest men in the world. His nine-hundred-year-old family was the founder of the European postal system. In his former duchy of Regensburg in Bavaria, where every citizen addresses the prince as "Your Excellency," he owns three castles, each one bigger than Buckingham Palace. Over on the other side of the pool, where all the news photographers have gathered, is Raquel Welch, another Brazil nut, who sometimes appears at a local nightclub doing her Vegas showroom act. Or you may see Marisa Berenson, Ursula Andress, Jacqueline Bisset. Or Orson Welles, one of the hotel's most legendary guests, who once, after a two-hour long distance phone spat with Dolores Del Rio, startled the management by hurling a chair through the French windows of his suite.

Just as you are tiring of star gazing, you behold a spectacle that fills you with an eerie sense of *déjà vu*. A wizened old bellman, attired in a baggy gray tunic with a red number embroidered on the collar, is walking around the patio holding forth a large slate. "Good God!" you think as you stare at the letters chalked on the board with a fine gothic hand, "He's summoning a guest to the phone!" Can you imagine anything so incredible in this day and age? No public address system bawling a call for *"Señor Perreira."* No sound at all. Only this old servant walking about with his mute slate. Take three! Thirty more frames of yellow celluloid.

When it's time for lunch, you get up from your vinyl beach mat and pull on your pants. If you had the confidence of the men you've been ogling, you'd throw on a robe; then, with scant concern for modesty, you'd pull down your trunks in front of everybody so you could wipe your damp ass with a towel. Next, you'd draw on tight white pants that would show a nice big bulge—which you would carefully adjust. Ah, the rich! They and the poor are on such familiar terms with their own bodies.

Now, you step out of the sun into the most charming luncheon restaurant in Rio. It's called the Pergola: a bright, riant birdcage woven of white lattice and trimmed with the orange color of the *abóbora*, the Brazilian pumpkin. The waiters are costumed to match the room: white tunics with shiny brass buttons down the center and bright blue trousers. On their epaulettes and splashed across their sleeves are broad stripes of the same pumpkin color that appears on the walls and pilasters. The order is taken by a maitre d'hotel who could be Re Momo, king of the Carnival. A jolly fat man with a well-practiced line of drolleries, he suggests outrageous quantities of rich food and makes a wry face if you order anything less than the full dose of heart-occluding cholesterol.

A typical dish is *picadinho*—chopped meat, highly spiced, served with a fried egg plopped on top and flanked with portions of fried plantains and sawdustlike farina. A tiny dish of spiced oil, in which float minnowy green peppers, completes this gut buster. The wine is Brazilian and better than most Californias. The dessert is so elaborate that you settle for an eclair and a *cafezinho*. By the time lunch is over, you're ready for a snooze, which you're surprised to learn is not a Brazilian custom, the Portuguese being such compulsive workers that even in the tropics they insist on plowing through the entire day and damn the heat!

In the late afternoon, at the cocktail hour, you descend to the brown leather interior of the bar, a soft, soothing atmosphere—like sitting inside an expensive purse. The walls are brown glass with white marbling, the fixtures Art Deco tinware. The drinks are *batidos*, the classic Brazilian mixed drink, composed of *cachaça* (white rum) and various mixers, like the heavily sweetened juice of the lime, peach, or *maracajas* (the passion fruit). At the end of the bar, you always find one of the regulars, like the portly American who calls himself Dr. Lowell, explaining at the same time that everybody in Rio calls himself "Doctor." Dr. Lowell conducts much of his business, whatever it may be, from the bar phone. When he isn't speaking into the instrument or swallowing his drink, he likes to reminisce about the days when Rio was a very provincial place and the Beach at Copacabana a distant retreat from the city.

When the evening rolls around, the presiding presence at the Copa appears with all the Beautiful People in town. He is Jorge Guinlé, last of the great playboys of the Western World, a delightful man and the most accomplished host in Rio. Jorge's family owns the hotel, and sometimes he lives in its residential annex with his constant companion, the model, Tanya Caldo. Jorge is a small, boyish figure, whose hair is beginning to show a few white threads but whose smile is sweet and youthful. He's always looking slightly amazed and exclaiming: "Fantastic!" Tanya is a classic Brazilian beauty. She has a broad cat face with a short nose and big dark eyes. Her mouth is like a bunny's. She exemplifies the extraordinary expressiveness of Latin women, always pouting,

staring, laughing, frowning, or teasing and flirting with Jorge who is as possessive of her as a high school boy with his first "steady." Tanya and Jorge are rarely alone, because Jorge assumes the burden of being a one-man tourist bureau for the rich and the famous. Ever since he was a very young playboy dating his first movie stars in Hollywood, Jorge has been unabashedly screen struck. The list of film celebrities he's schlepped down to Rio would extend to the end of this chapter. It is said that in his palatial home in Teresópolis, he has a photomontage of all the movie queens he's conquered.

The first time I met Jorge, he was arranging his party at a long table in the bar. He had Margaux Hemingway and her husband, Ross Wetson; the novelist Harold Robbins; the jazz producer, Norman Granz and his wife; the Hollywood talent manager and promoter, Allan Carr; an ex-Dior model named Martine; and a good-looking couple from California. I was very impressed with this covey of jet-setters, until I tuned in on the conversation. Conversation is not really the word: I mean chatter. There were only three topics, I soon discovered. They kept gabbing about where they had been, what they had done for fun, and what they had bought at Bloomingdale's. There may have been some other topic they touched upon, but I doubt it. Apparently everybody did a great deal of travelling, but everywhere they went they always ended up in the same place: Regine's. The Dior model, who had classic features and a very impressive bust, was recently divorced and in search of a fresh husband. In the course of the next week, she must have encountered every rich and powerful man in Rio. She was always keyed up as if she were on speed, and the narrative of her adventures was very entertaining.

One night she was picked up in great style by a Brazilianaire. She was sitting with some friends at a table in a club when the waiter appeared with a costly bottle of Dom Perignon. He explained that it had been sent by the gentleman "over there." Turning to see her generous admirer, she spotted a very dark, good-looking man, in his forties, smiling through the murk with flashing white teeth. Nodding and beckoning, the model invited the gentleman to her table. He appeared instantly and was soon deep in conversation with her. As the first bottle of wine began to run low, another bottle appeared and soon another. Eventually, the man, who was a big wheel in the local construction industry, swept the whole party up and took them out with him for a night on the town. He had a limousine waiting at the curbside with a driver, but he insisted on their going to his garage, where he had three other cars brought out until they could reach his prized Mercedes, worth in Rio about $75,000. Getting behind the wheel of this mint-condition status symbol, he began a round of festivities that lasted till dawn and brought the model back to the Palace with her motors running at turbine velocity. "I loved the way he kept dragging those cars out of the garage!" she gasped. "It was just like he couldn't find his favorite shirt—not this one! Or this one! Or this one!" But he did manage to show the foreigners all his camels.

Beki Klabin's Penthouse Party

During Carnival the wealthy and distinguished Cariocas vie with one another in assembling glamorous guests in no less glamorous settings. Pitanguy, the best known of Rio's many plastic surgeons, has a home with lavish tropical gardens that is always the site of a celebrity-studded afternoon party. Jorge Guinlé, who had for many years the most beautiful apartment in Rio, in the Flamengo district, close to the city, used to give a splendid party before the annual Municipal Ball. Or you may be invited to a penthouse party. Rio is a city of lavish high-rises with terraces that command breathtaking views. A couple of years ago, I attended an afternoon affair given by Beki Klabin—Rio's most publicized society lady and the first wealthy, socially prominent matron to parade with a samba school.

The ex-wife of an immensely wealthy industrialist, Beki is a Sephardic Jew whose family came to Brazil from Turkey. Once she was the mistress of a mansion, but today she prefers the light housekeeping of a stunning penthouse in Ipanema. Stepping off the lift, you encounter a plate glass door—which I almost walked through. Loud samba music is playing from within and you have to bang and shout until someone hears you. The apartment is straight out of the pages of an international edition of *Vogue* or *Harper's Bazaar*. The decorating scheme called for silver and blue and by God, everything you see is either royal blue or silver—pure silver. Everywhere you look you see silver bowls freighted with silver fruits standing on silver trays surrounded by silver utensils, silver baubles, silver chatzkahs.

Beki receives you on the patio, a white marble terrace that wraps around two sides of the building and contains a number of umbrella-shaded tables and a small, circular swimming pool lined with blue plastic and raised on several steps like an altar to the god, Tanga. The view over the white parapet is awesome: It ranges from one end of Ipanema to the other—from the Two Brothers (twin volcanic peaks standing up like the tips of crossed fingers) out across the ocean studded with hump-backed stony isles, to the conical rock of Arpoador.

Beki is seated at a table drinking a *coco batido* (vodka in coconut milk), out of a little glass. A small, dark, Semitic-looking woman with long, stringy hair, wearing a gray tank suit, she turns a face toward you like those loved by Modigliani. Masklike, the face is comprised of three ovals: a perpendicular oval crossed by the horizontal ovals. Her immense eyes are made even more prominent by the long artificial lashes that fringe them. Beki is known to you only as a notorious publicity hound: Instinctively, you are disposed to dislike her. She disarms you instantly, however, by recounting the story of her involvement with Portela with an engaging mixture of ingenuousness, shrewdness, and *joie de vivre*.

Like many wealthy matrons, she grew bored with life after her children were married and her own marriage had been outlived. Instead of sinking into the apathy of middle age, she decided to seek excitement by violating the taboo against public exposure that makes the wives of Brazilian millionaires live like harem concubines. First, she appeared on TV, doing an interview show that became a great favorite in Rio's kitchens, where the mistress often joins the maids to watch the *novellas*, or soap operas. Having enjoyed the notoriety that the TV show provided, she decided to give the taboos an even more violent jolt by going out on the streets to jump with a samba school. She chose Portela for this purpose both because it was the greatest of the schools and because its colors—blue and white—matched her own. Seeking to establish with the school a rapport that would soothe everybody's sensibilities—fearing the *sambistas* might think she was patronizing them and fearing just as much that they would view her as a rich mark—she contrived a couple of sensational parties. They were thrown both at her penthouse and at her son's larger and more lavish home in the Largo do Boticária (a delightful enclave of quaintly decorated nineteenth-century houses high in the mountains overlooking the city in a place that resembles a stage setting for *The Barber of Seville*). They brought together, on the one side, the sophisticated members of Rio's jet set and, on the other, the poor but proud folk who comprised the samba school.

The idea of Natal and his black henchmen lolling about in La Klabin's penthouse and mansion, making the *batacuda* with their jungle drums and dancing, perhaps obscenely, with one of Rio's wealthiest society matrons excited the Brazilian media to madness. Articles, stories, shows began appearing right and left, reporting, exposing, scolding, ridiculing, and fictionalizing the exploits of Beki among the *bambas*. It was like Tom Wolfe's "Radical Chic": New York's high society hobnobbing with the Black Panthers. But where New Yorkers paid scant attention to the event until it was caricatured in Wolfe's bitchy prose, the Cariocas followed the story's unfolding as they would some sensational scandal in the government. Rio is a *very* small town.

As the time for Carnival approached, Beki began to prepare methodically for her appearance. She commissioned her dress designer, Evandro de Castro Lima, King of Carnival Costumes, to make her a magnificent *fantasia*. Beki was to appear as a *destaque*. She required a huge eighteenth-century ballgown in stunning white, all hand embroidered, with a billowing skirt covered with maribou feathers and a great headpiece crowned with a glory of white plumes. Four seamstresses labored for two months on this Cinderella costume. Eventually, all the pieces were conveyed to Evandro's atelier, where they were stitched together under the master's watchful eye.

When the gown was ready, Beki donned it repeatedly to practice her samba steps. She wore her white slippers around the house to soften them. When the night of the parade arrived, she took her two best maids and the gown and repaired to the offices of the Diner's Club (a family business of which she is vice-president) near the *pista*, where she spent three hours putting on her makeup and costume. Getting dressed at home was out of the question. "How would I get into the lift?" she exclaims when you make the foolish suggestion. (In a recent soap opera starring an actress who looks exactly like Beki, the wealthy society lady who is to dance in the Carnival parade is hoisted off her penthouse terrace in full regalia by one of Rio's ubiquitous construction cranes.)

Only when Beki had walked to the staging area behind the Candelaria church did the audacity of her decision begin to trouble her. Then she developed a bad case of stage fright. "I thought to myself, 'I can't do this! I'm crazy! I can't move my legs!' Then, after I took the first steps, I heard the crowd shouting, 'Beki! Beki!' Suddenly, I felt so wonderful, I couldn't stop. When we came to the end of the *pista*, I said, 'Is that all there is? I can't wait for next year!'"

Carnival Commences

Carnival commences officially at twelve noon on the Saturday before Ash Wednesday. At that moment out of their clubhouse in downtown Rio come bumping and strutting the members of Rio's oldest Carnival club, the Balo Preto, or "Black Ball," an organization that traces its roots beyond the samba schools to the turn of the century. Into the blazing hot sun of noonday Rio prance the members, jumping behind their hot little band. A symbolic six blocks they march; then, they break up and dash back to their air-conditioned clubhouse inside a high-rise office building. Carnival has commenced—but nobody except a few officials and news photographers is aware of the fact.

The real beginning of the public festivities is nine or ten the same night, when the first major carnival parade comes up the Avenida Presidente Vargas, a vast space-age Napoleonic boulevard bulldozed straight as an arrow through the heart of downtown Rio and lined with towering quadrangular glass and concrete office buildings. The boulevard ends with the beautiful seventeenth-century Candelaria Church, which served for many years as the marshaling point and illuminated backdrop for the Carnival parades. Then, Rio began to build a subway, and construction commenced right at the point where the major parades were staged. The result was that the city decided to move the festivities out along the avenue into the area of the old Mangue redlight district, which was being demolished. As there had been many complaints in the past about the size and accommodations of the temporary stands, the city took the opportunity presented by the relocation of the parades to design and build the greatest street stadium in history.

To appreciate the problem presented by the *arquibancadas*, the "reviewing stands," one has to grasp the enormous scale of the parades. The biggest parade, that of the samba schools, which takes place on Sunday night, commences around ten o'clock and may extend to the following day at noon—or even later! During that time a minimum of ten and sometimes as many as fourteen samba schools will pass in review. Each school marshalls about 2,500 costumed performers plus a great array of floats, portable stages, and other show-biz properties. An hour must be allotted for the school to dance the length of *pista*, of 980 meters, better than half a mile. Between each school there are long pauses while the next school gets into position to go on. Sometimes as much as an hour elapses without anything happening "on stage." The upshot is that the street stadium must be constructed in such a way as to provide temporary housing for a great number of people, who are going to not only watch a fourteen-hour show but in the process perform most of their natural functions, including a great deal of eating and drinking.

In 1976, RioTur, the agency that rules the Carnival, decided that it would spend 3.5 million dollars on a street stadium with a capacity of eighty thousand spectators. The stands were erected on steel supports to a height of about five stories, with built-in bars, lavatories, fire engine and ambulance stations, and an immensely complicated wiring job, like that of a battleship, for the lights, sound system, and the various public media, which carry this all-important event all over Brazil by radio and TV and by movie camera and satellite to the rest of the world. Twenty thousand seats are distributed gratis to the general public; and the rest are sold at prices that range up to a couple of hundred dollars for a box. Obtaining a good seat often involves last-minute negotiations with hotel concierges or ticket scalpers who haunt the tourist district. The biggest problem faced by the visitor is not obtaining the ticket but sustaining himself through the all-night ordeal.

The secret is either to arm yourself with stimulants or to practice the art of catnapping between parades. The punishment for leaving early is the loss of opportunity to see some of the best schools, which for reasons that are hard to understand invariably appear at the end of the parade. One of the strangest experiences of Carnival is watching Rio's blood-red dawn coming up the avenue after a night of hallucinatory spectacles. The designers of the Carnival pageants will capitalize on the fact that their groups are scheduled to appear in daylight and clothe their people in colors or metals that will glint with extraordinary effect in the bright morning sunshine.

Even when the parades are not passing down the *pista*, the thousands of people in the stands are never idle. This is their great annual all-night party. They busy themselves with eating and drinking. No matter how long the parade lasts, even if it be twenty-four hours long, there is never a moment when Rio's relentless soft-drink, beer, ice cream, and sandwich peddlers (the same guys who destroy the oceanside tranquillity of the beaches at Copacabana and Ipanema) are not climbing indefatigably up and down the stands with their boxes and barrels slung across their shoulders and their money folded across their knuckles like old-time crap shooters. Shrilling out "Sandweechas!" or the beery cry of "*Cerveja!*", they keep everybody's mouth full all night long. Their most bizarre offerings are soft drinks in plastic bottles shaped like fruits: orange squash in bright plastic oranges, grape soda in bunches of purple plastic grapes, or any soft drink in a long squeeze bottle like a shampoo flask. Imagine the picture presented by eighty thousand people, all of whom are sucking, squeezing, biting, and gnawing on grotesquely shaped baby bottles whose nipples have been snipped off by the vendors' scissors!

Another great source of entertainment in the *arquibancadas* is mass singing. Brazilians are instinctive choristers. Someone will strike up one of the hits of the Carnival and instantly a whole section will erupt in song. Triggering this sing-along relflex is one of the goals of every samba school. Just to make sure that everybody knows the words, the school will distribute thousands of slips of paper (or little fans) with the text before its appearance. Often as not, the spectators sing the samba better than the dancers in the street, giving it that tremendous rhythmic verve it demands, while doing a hot samba in a space the size of a handkerchief. When the *sambistas* come singing and dancing down the avenue, they sweep up the crowd, until it seems like the whole city is following them, like the children of Hamlin traipsing after the Pied Piper. The ultimate accolade the crowd can bestow on a school is to chant, "*ja gagnou! ja gagnou!*"—"You've got it made!"

The worst thing that ever happens at Carnival is that on the night of the great parade it rains! Rio's notorious *chuva* is the

theme of countless Carnival songs, and when it descends on the samba schools, these gallant performers must carry on with the show. No matter how many millions of dollars worth of costumes are spoiled by being dragged through puddles, no matter that the plumes droop, the makeup runs and the drums give forth only a soggy, muffled beat, the show must go on. You can't postpone Christmas!

Normally, the only problems on parade nights are those created by last-minute altercations between clubs and officials or by the inevitable marshalling delays. When the spectators, far more tolerant than most, have decided that they have waited long enough, they start to pound their feet rhythmically and make their impatience audible. What they would do if they really got angry is anybody's guess. In the old days, pitched battles were the rule, not the exception, at Carnival. Today, order is maintained by the conspicuous presence of the Brazilian army's tough-looking riot-control squads. They wear German army fatigue caps, black boots, green uniforms, and carry long hollow metal truncheons. The contrast between the ecstatic *sambistas* and these grim warders is highly suggestive. It reminds you that behind the joyous ebullience of the Brazilian people lies the terrifying power of a police state.

The first-night parade is essentially a warm-up. About ten in the evening, when the stands are only half full, the sound of a razzy jazzy band is heard bumping up the boulevard. Instantly the crowd is on its feet, ready to cheer the leading marchers. Heading the parade is Re Momo, the King of Carnival, and his entourage. A fat, middle-aged man in a tired looking costume, Re Momo is a Fellini buffoon monarch resigned to his role, ruling Carnival like a weary, sated Caesar, tired of it all. If the king is more amusing than exciting, the same cannot be said of his court. A metaphysical shudder passes through you when you glimpse this rout of death's heads and demons dancing with hot samba queens and prancing cockhorses. In a flash, you recognize the ancient Mediterranean philosophy that made the Romans crown the banquet table with a skeleton: the profoundly ironic conjunction of *mors et amor*, the link of love and death.

Sunday night is the night of nights, the climax of the entire year. During the preceding week, thousands of *sambistas* have been working round the clock, taking pills to stay awake. Though some of them have had thirty or forty years of experience in preparing these pageants, there is always the familiar show-biz crisis just before opening night. The costumes don't fit, the *alegorias* are too big to go through the factory door, the sound equipment fails at the final rehearsal. On the afternoon before the parade, a squad of officials is despatched to the *pista* to take a reading on last-minute conditions. Then, about four hours before kickoff time, the manically excited performers begin to arrive at the marshalling point in cars and buses.

When the time arrives for the school to march up the parade route, the *bateria* unlimbers its drums and strikes up the beat. The only solemn people in the entire city, the drummers, give an impression of intense concentration and abstraction from the event. They seem burdened by their responsibility for keeping the beat, which is, from the ritual standpoint, the most momentous of all the duties that must be discharged in the ceremony. To inspire the *bateria* to play with fervor, the school will generally put out in front of them during the warm-up some of the most enticing *bundas* in the city. While these girls throw their meat like burlesque queens, the drummers frown intently and beat their instruments.

Finally the *comissão de frente* appears and takes its place at the head of the marchers. The title float is wheeled into position. The parade marshalls run up and down the ranks verifying that every *ala* is in place. The directors in their natty blazers and snap-brim hats flourish their swagger sticks. Tension builds like an airplane straining at the end of the runway. Then, with a shrill blast on a traffic whistle, the *sambistas* march off into the blazing lights of the avenue and the crowd's huzzahs.

There is nothing—no film, no show, no event of any description—that compares with the spectacle of the samba schools on parade. The effect of seeing a school first appear advancing down the avenue is sublime. Picture the scene. It is late at night, perhaps three o'clock in the morning. Already you have seen so many thousands of costumed figures, heard so much samba *batucuda*, seen so much solo dancing and *destaques* and *alegorias* that you feel utterly drained, listless, and sleepy. Then a palpable stir runs up and down the stands.

The sound of the big drums comes like the crashing of distant surf or the awesome thump of a distant piledriver. The spectators strain to see the distant marchers, standing in their places, and gazing up the avenue over the heads of the people in front. They are looking up a tunnel of bright lights drilled through the dark night and lined, like the wings of an old-fashioned stage, with an endless perspective of brilliantly painted and internally illuminated flats. At the far end of this long tunnel, they now discern the first units of the school slowly advancing. They know there must be singing but not a word can be heard. Advancing with glacierlike slowness, yet with a sense of irresistible onset, they finally come close enough so that the spectators can see past the first *alas* to those behind and those behind those. By the time the procession gets within earshot, it is possible to see dozens of ranks of elaborately costumed and gorgeously colored performers stretching back for as much as half a mile. They flood the avenue from side to side like a river of color. As they draw closer, they pass and repass, doing the snake dance, each *ala* in a different costume with color contrasts that make the river of many hues like layers of differently tinted sands in a glass. Finally, the spectators are greeted with a close-up of the first wing and the first

float announcing the name of the school and the title of the pageant. If it is a great school with a good designer, the effect may be brilliant: an immense architectural fantasy containing all manner of interesting sculptures, lighting effects, symbols, and joyous *sambistas* dancing, singing, and hailing the crowd.

At the same time the beat of the music becomes much louder. Straining a look up the street, you see a formidable battery approaching, beating before it, like game birds rising in a field, wildly soaring dancers, the most frenzied in the pageant, writhing and leaping nakedly in the very teeth of the band. Band? It sounds more like an enormous machine: a harvesting combine, a cement mixer, a massive paving apparatus thundering and hissing up the avenue, ringed by the halations of its shiny tin instruments.

Restricted to pure percussion, the *escolas* generate the power for their immense pageants by increasing the number and variety of instruments to astronomical proportions. Twenty ranks of twenty players may pass by, hammering, scraping, socking, rattling, and pumping as many different devices: tin shakers flashing on high look like new potato graters; gypsy tambourines jingling and flying around the players' heads, shoulders, and hips; frying pans and serving plates clattering like kitchen mayhem; serrated cow horns and bamboo sticks rasping and grating; resin-rubbed *cuicas* groaning and dozens of *tamborims* crepitating like heat lightning around the deep, hollow thunder of the silver, cylindrical *surdos*.

Once the first pageants in the dusk-to-dawn parade flow by, a pattern can be discerned amidst their apparent anarchy. First, there is the courtly salutation: perhaps, "The academicians of Salgueiro greet the people of Rio, the media of television, radio, and press, and present the *Visit of the King of the Congo to Recife* [a north coast city] requesting permission to pass through." Then, a line of old blacks approaches, dressed to the nines in five-button Savile Row suits, with brown derbies, spats, gloves, and canes. Wheeling around to the public, they doff their hats, bow gravely, and retire to the sidelines to watch the parade pass by. Instantly, the samba strikes up and a score of fat old peasant women in the dress of Bahia pass by, tropical fruits piled on their kerchiefed heads, hoop skirts billowing, chains, amulets, necklaces jingling, as they skim back and forwards across the street as if propelled on wheels.

After these follow the standard bearer and the major domo, figures of eighteenth-century Meissen ware: she a mulato Marie Antoinette, smiling radiantly and twirling gaily with her school's banner; he a tall, skinny-shanked black, in powdered wig and white satin knee breeches, partnering his lady and then cutting away to do an elaborate parody of courtly manners, with cross-legged hesitation steps and nimble turns flagged to sudden stops

ARI' E LALA'

with flutters of his lace fan. Pouring along now come rank after rank of gorgeously costumed Harlequins and Pierrots and Noble Savages and Fruit Vendors and Plantation Belles and Old Crones and Conquistadors and Fisher Folk and Dumas Musketeers, all in the red and white or rose and green of the *escola*. Toward the end the theme is exalted in a grand finale and apotheosis. A towering float approaches, bearing the biggest, blackest man in Rio—the King of the Congo. As this giant graciously salutes the crowd, his entourage swings into sight bearing all the wealth of Africa. Leopard and tiger skins jounce by on poles, deep-slung ivory tusks swing between naked bearers, broad trays of gold and gems ride high on the heads of slaves, giant warriors clad in iridescent feathers do slow flings, harem-bedecked slave girls wince under the whips of overseers, and last of all, a herd of stiff-legged, long-necked giraffes scampers by, each beast with a little peephole in its breast.

All through the long haul, from the first waves to the last, the paraders have been singing their samba. Indistinct at first, then slowly emerging—like a picture from a developing bath—one melodic contour, one verse at a time, until now the crowd has caught the tune and words, a bouncy, square-cut song, ebullient as a football march. The thousands along the parade route join the dancers in singing their new samba, bringing the procession to a huge tribal climax—"Oh la la, Oh, le, le, everyone is welcome, everyone must join us!"

The stars of Carnival are, primarily, the women. As their bodies and erotic dancing constitute one of the most enduring and vivid impressions of the festival, it is easy to come away with the idea that Carnival is essentially a glorified orgy. It is an orgy—an orgy of exhibitionism and narcissism. All year long, maids, laundresses, and sewing machine operators labor at their tasks and live either behind the kitchens of the rich or in the hovels of the poor. They gaze compulsively at television and dream the ancient dream of Cinderella. Then, one night, they are transformed into that legendary creature the *mulata*, the *morena*, the brown-skinned gal who is the queen of Carnival, the theme of every song, the envy of every woman, the lust of every man.

On this night the nameless, faceless housemaid or seamstress is transported to a dream theater and set before a vast throng of cheering, ogling, and huzzahing spectators. She responds, instinctively, from the very depth of her being with everything that is most alluring about her as a woman. Opening her arms wide in the classic samba gesture, as if to embrace the world; flashing that sunburst smile that transfigures the human face; spreading her thighs as if to admit a lover; arching up her tail, decorated perhaps with a flamboyant spray of bird feathers, this *pastora*, this "shepherdess," as the quaint language of Carnival designates her, begins a bold, sensual advance that soon has her ample flesh shaking on her bones in an ecstatic quivering and shimmering and shimmying that has the crowd roaring and the sombre riot police smiling wickedly and the photographers bouncing in the street before her with their flashbulbs exploding like popcorn in a hot frying pan.

The Carnival Balls

Second in importance only to the pageants of the *escolas de samba* are the great society balls of the Carnival season. They combine the costumed glamour and erotic intrigue of their ancestor, the Venetian masked ball, with the seething ecstasy of the modern discotheque. Melding the romping ebullience and the innocent gaiety of a country dance with the decadent *triste tropique* air of the debauched planter in the jungle, the balls reek of wealth, class, and chic, yet frequently they descend to the level of the "group grope" or the raunchy slum party. The rich white aristocracy's answer to the revels of the black masses, the swank parody of black soul that corresponds to the samba school's parody of the panache of the old imperial court, the society ball is the flip side of the Carnival coin.

There are countless balls at this time in Rio, but the first important society ball is held a week before Carnival in a vast gala tent on the grounds of the yacht club, which looks out over the boats anchored in beautiful Botafogo Bay. The prime attraction of the ball is not, however, the decor or the scenery: This ball is one of the great sex events of Carnival and is attended by most of Rio's prosperous bachelors and husbands. Unaccompanied by wives or girl friends, they go to meet the most beautiful girls of the city, who respond to the provocation of the occasion by wearing and doing some pretty crazy things, like tearing off their clothes and leaping into the pool naked.

Until recently, the greatest of the balls, the Municipal Ball, was held at the opera house—a bumpy, lumpy old beaux arts monument crusted with ancient grime and located right in the midst of the merrymakers on the Rio Branco. On the night of the ball, the Municipal was ringed with a crack unit of the Brazilian army, togged out for the occasion in white jackets and chrome steel helmets. They formed a human wall around the opera house, holding automatic rifles with fixed bayonets. If any of the local slum bums took a notion to meddle with his betters, he would soon have been reduced to chopped meat. To further increase the security of this great congregation of Brazilian notables, a high wire fence was erected around the entrance and a whole series of checkpoints were established at which various parts of the tickets—the size of breakfast napkins—were torn off. Finally, after passing through this maze and walking up a sort of gangplank, it was at last possible to step across the threshold and into the palace of pleasure.

Inside the building, one felt like he had stepped onto a set for *The Grand Duchess of Gerolstein*. Rising before him like a marble cataract was a grand staircase that paused halfway up in its imposing ascent to rest on a landing, where the steps parted abruptly, like dancers in a minuet, and then, after executing a U-turn, rose again steeply toward the mezzanine. At the point of partition, a flying goddess stood, like an Olympian major domo, ordering the guests to the right and the left with a gesture of her outthrust arm. A tremendous crowd of luxuriously and bizarrely clad figures was crawling up and down the stairs, one stream seeking to ascend while the other struggled just as determinedly to come down from the heights above. Instead of the costumes for which this setting had been originally contrived—the gleaming top hats, flouncy gowns and shawls and diamond tiaras of the opera aristocracy—this crowd looked like a gaggle of extras milling about on a Hollywood back lot.

At the foot of the stairs might be a boy gotten up as an angel, with rolls of carrot-colored paper hair crowned by an elegant little halo sustained from the back of his head by a slender wire. His face was covered with clown white and speckled with brightly colored confetti. Beside him stood a swarthy Indian prince in a stunning costume of white satin. The sash of his elegant jacket had been tossed with supreme casualness (doubtless crossed and recrossed twenty or thirty times to get the perfect hang). His superb turban was gauded with a glittering jewel and topped with a feathery and immaculate plume that rose from the top of his head like a puff of steam. Across from the raja stood an African queen, with a huge bush of bristly black hair, wearing a leopard skin that had been slung provocatively across her breasts and muscular thighs, leaving totally bare her thick strong legs and toes of prehensile articulation. The most unforgettable figure on this human totem pole was a dissolute old Caesar whose profile suggested a human coin: bold aquiline nose, massive bald head, fringe of dyed, *frisured* hair, and then the crowning touch—a splendid wreath of gold laurel leaves.

As this phantasmagoric spectacle overwhelmed one's visual sensibilities, his auditory nerves, especially where they lace up over the top of the skull, were crushed by the thunderous downward pressure of jungle drums, thumping out an Amazonian beat with the thick rank atmosphere of Manaus and Belém steaming up from every stroke. Mounting in the direction of these drums, one reached the upstairs lobby; its elegant marble floor was thickly mulched with cracked plastic glasses, crumpled paper napkins, greasy chicken bones, and splayed champagne corks. Still searching for the source of the music, one might open the door to a box on the Golden Horseshoe and get an eyeful of glamour. In the box itself might be a party of richly clad aristocrats: a gallant old boy with white hair wings dressed in a dinner jacket and flanked by a ravishingly beautiful young girl in a white jersey cling gown (totally innocent of underwear) and another youthful figure dressed all in white: a grinning, japing, monkey-faced little gay boy in a suede frontier costume outlined in fringes. The master was supervising the labors of a waiter in a white jacket with gold-braided epaulets, who was removing from a wine bucket a spent bottle of champagne while he replaced it with a fresh bottle. Without a moment's hesitation, the master would offer you an empty champagne glass and beckon the waiter to fill it.

Looking out the front of the box, you gazed down on the floor and stage of the opera house. The spectacle went far beyond anything you had ever seen at the movies. The stage floor had been extended out over the seats of the orchestra to make the entire ground floor of the theater an immense dance hall. The ceilings, walls, and box fronts had been decorated lavishly with vividly painted flats and hangings. On the dance floor was a densely packed mob that looked as though it could move only on a vertical not a lateral axis. Every once in a while the music would reach a peak, and the dancers would all jump into the air and shout. The music, which was now extremely loud and palpably vibrating the old building, was being supplied by two orchestras which were installed, one on either side of the dance floor. The band on the left was playing a fast choo-choo samba, with the beat laid out across the snares and a couple of old blacks whacking their bass drums with leather-headed cannibal sticks. The melody was intoned stridently by a whole rank of white society trumpet players: the kind that raise their knees as they strain at the high notes, giving the impression that they are bringing the sounds up from the bottom of their jockey shorts.

As always at Carnival, the principal players in the ball game are women: in this case, the young, beautiful, pampered wives and daughters of the richest men in the country. These wealthy, well-educated, widely traveled, and highly sophisticated ladies behave at a ball no differently than would their cooks and maids. In fact, it is often virtually impossible to distinguish the light-skinned whores from society girls. In either case, the goal is precisely the same—to star for one night as a sex queen. Indeed, everything the women do at these events, either by way of preparation or participation, can be viewed as a calculated erotic performance.

The first step for such women is to assure themselves of making the biggest possible splash by appearing on television and in all the Carnival magazines. To achieve this, they need one of the prime settings at the ball. Ordinary tickets provide nothing more than admission to the ball. For a prime location, a party must be formed and a table or a box reserved. A table at a big ball might be worth $500 plus the cost of food and drink. A box goes for about $2,500, but the great thing about a box is that it provides the classic see-and-be-seen setting. Belles can make a great effect by sitting on the box edge all night with their beautiful legs hanging down like those flouncy dolls designed to be propped up against bed bolsters. For maximum effect, however, five or six ladies should adorn the box front—all identically costumed. Naturally it is very important that this chorus line be nicely matched in age, color, and beauty.

To turn for the moment to the vital question of what a Carioca belle should wear to the ball, it may be said that over the years there has been a very pronounced evolution—or perhaps, more appropriately, *devolution*—in the costumes of society ladies. In the old days women wore elaborate and costly ball gowns that threw the primary visual accent on their faces. Then as the cult of body worship developed and the new jet-set morality was introduced into Rio society, the style changed and women began to copy what they saw in American girlie magazines and the more risqué types of show-biz costumes. In 1971, when I first attended the Municipal Ball, the look was part harem concubine and part Tahitian surf sweetie. The standard outfit was a long skirt in two panels, slashed to the hips, showing only a tiny pair of flesh-colored pants and a skimpy bra. Within a few years, many women had discarded the skirt and appeared in costumes that were glorified versions of the bikini. Now the bikini has been discarded in favor of the even more revealing *tanga*, and the bra has been tossed aside with a sigh of liberation in favor of a couple of tasseled pasties over the nipples.

While women's costumes have steadily dwindled toward the implicit goal of well-painted nudity, the costumes of another, much older, group of revelers have evolved in precisely the opposite direction. At some time well after midnight, when the dancers are sorely in need of rest, the music will stop and the master of ceremonies will announce an exhibition of *fantasias de luxo*. This fashion show of the world's most elaborate and costly costumes is one of the most bizarre features of Carnival. It is a natural development of Carnival's aspect as masquerade, but the lengths to which the designs have been carried in recent years have made the principal shows spectacles that could be conceived only by a Carioca.

Only in Brazil could one find a whole village in the interior where the women are willing to work all year long for petty wages doing complicated embroidery for Carnival costumes. Only in Brazil could one buy great quantities of rubies, emeralds, topazes, and aquamarines to sew on a king's robes for prices less than a king's ransom. Only in Brazil could one find enough skilled lapidaries to polish these stones and mount them so that they can be sewn to capes and trains and doublets or mounted on crowns.

Even Brazil, however, cannot supply the ostrich feathers that must be brought from India or the glittering crystals that are made only in France. Then there is gold, many ounces of it, which must be fabricated into embroidery, ornaments, and even great sculptural objects like crowns. Even in Brazil it costs a great deal of money to dress like His Serene Highness, the Czar of All the Russias.

Who is crazy enough to try? Who would put up the money, take such pains, and assume the burden of such a colossal act of overdressing? The answer is that Rio has a circle of costume freaks who are as familiar to the public as pop singers, television personalities, or soccer stars. These men and women (mostly they are men) receive more publicity at Carnival season than any other group of carnivalers. Nor is theirs merely a local fame. The best of them compete all over Brazil at Carnival time: a week before Carnival at Recife; a week after that at São Paulo; and in the crowded four days and three nights of Carnival, they have nightly exhibitions in Rio. When Carnival concludes, they go on tour as a show, with a supporting cast and a manager. In the course of the year they may play as many as 240 dates, ranging all over South America and as far north as Miami, with its huge Cuban community. These top performers call themselves "The Conquerers of the *Fantasia*," and they regard their work as a monumental contribution to the glory of the Motherland. The greatest of them points with pride to his old costumes, which are on exhibit in places as distant as Paris and New York. What he longs for is a museum of Carnival, where these splendid clothes can be enshrined permanently like the robes of the Czar in the Kremlin or the vestments of the Pope in the Vatican.

This hero of Carnival is the fascinating and droll Clovis Bornay, who is in real life a curator of Rio's Historical Museum. A striking-looking man, with a fleshy but handsome face, the bold nose of a Roman emperor, bleached hair, and the most expressive eyes in Rio, Clovis, as everybody calls him, is one of the most scholarly and dedicated men ever to sally forth to a ball accoutred as an Indian Maharajah and riding atop an elephant! Always smiling and bursting at Carnival with radiant looks that range from wicked glances to provocative stares to madly leering gazes like those of a manic moth—looks that kill his audiences and bring them screaming to their feet shouting, "Clovis! Clovis!" the Conqueror of the *Fantasia* is as much an actor as he is a great male model.

His arch-rival in the competitions is Beki Klabin's friend, Evandro de Castro Lima, the couturier. Evandro is rather more sedate as a personality, but his *fantasias* are if anything even more pompous and flamboyant than Clovis's. Evandro wins a lot of first prizes and appears on a lot of magazine covers. Yet it is Clovis who enjoys the prestige and esteem of this curious art form, which is relished in Rio even by the coarsest sorts of workers and all the old *macho* types. Traditionally, Carnival meant masquerade; in spending an entire year preparing the most stunning costume imaginable, Clovis and Evandro and the rest of the Conquerors are really performing an act of piety, sustaining a tradition, fulfilling an obligation that has now become a trust and a patriotic exercise, honored by the public and press, as one pays homage to a man who has undertaken a very difficult duty on behalf of his country.

The final stage in the year-long quest for the winning costume—a campaign that entails many preliminary battles with seamstresses, tailors, customs officials (who are entitled to slap incredible duties on imported luxuries such as feathers), and the press, which is always trying to suss out this year's design and publicize it—is the elaborate ritual entailed in donning the huge costume.

Five full hours are required to put on a *fantasia de luxo*. The model must be assisted by several dressers and he must be skillfully made up by a maquillage artist. The first step is a perfumed bath to which has been added special salts that brace the body for the coming ordeal. Then the face is iced to firm the skin for the application of cosmetics. Most costumes require false beards, moustaches, eyelashes, and wigs. Next, the model is strapped into a steel corset which is fitted with hooks and armatures which hold the garment in precisely the right alignment with the body. As the costumes are usually both heavy and bulky, they are lined with foam rubber to give them body. Invariably, a train is worn and a huge headdress that may extend several feet above the model's head. Often, buildings or animals or whole groups of figures are constructed into which the model is embedded.

When the model has finally been accoutred, he is a very vulnerable creature. Covered from head to foot in emeralds, rubies, and other precious stones, often he requires a police escort. Wearing a costume that makes him much larger than life, he must be conveyed to the exhibition in a truck or at least an open car. Even when delivered safely to the club or theater, he must beware of thoughtless well-wishers who will damage his outfit with an impulsive embrace. Of jealous rivals, eager to sabotage his costume, he must be particularly wary.

Clovis Bornay has been exhibiting since 1937. In that time he has built up a remarkable gallery of effigies, which he has catalogued in big color photographs. Unlike Evandro, the couturier, who is concerned mostly with making a splash with a costume that is a free rendering of some exotic theme, Clovis, the curator, labors to make his costumes accurate historically, down to the smallest detail. Two outfits based on the style of a king at the eighteenth-century French court illustrate the range of his art. One costume is titled "Louis XV"; the other, "His Majesty, the Samba."

Louis XV, as Clovis Bornay sees him, was an elegant fag. His court costume is distinguished by elegance of line, suavity of material, richness of ornamentation without gaudiness, and exquisiteness of detailing. The basic costume is knee breeches and a frock coat of white satin. The knee breeches are very tight fitting, with flat ribbon bows just below the knee. The white silk hose reveal finely shaped calves. The shoes are pumps with small heels, like women's slippers, endorsed with bows and square, jeweled buckles. The coat is cream-colored satin with big, broad cuffs ending in gold lace. Gold and jeweled appliqués adorn the cuffs and the front of the coat. A broad gold-and-jeweled sash, slashes across the breast, terminating in a huge round ornament and tassel. Under the chin is a high stock with a gold lace jabot. On the hands, silk gloves with the fingertips cut off and jeweled rings on the fingers. A white silky wig is tied in back with a black bow. The crown is Grecian: a mass of gold encrustation bedizened with small rubies. The cloak is long and black with ermine trim and satin lining. A broad ermine cape collar backs the head. Makeup is very effeminate with white skin, pronounced pink lipstick, a dark mole on the upper right cheek bone, the eyebrows lined boldly to frame the beautiful eyes. The king holds a staff about five feet long, gold, with a fretted ball at the end and in the middle, a satin ribbon.

This costume involves relatively little exaggeration of the authentic designs. It is simply more luxurious and elegant than its prototype. "His Majesty, The Samba" goes to the opposite extreme in stylizing the costume of the eighteenth-century French king. A travesty on the traditional outfit worn by the *mestre-salas* of the samba schools, this design mocks good-humoredly the garish magnificence that typifies the Negro's taste in Carnival finery.

The makeup for the costume is blackface with silver paint outlining the eyes and the huge red mouth. The components are essentially the same as those for "Louis XV," but everything has been grossly exaggerated and caricatured. There are also some significant substitutions. Instead of the slender, elegant walking staff held by Louis XV (a stick that is at once a courtier's wand of office and the rococo shepherd's crook) "His Majesty, The Samba" carries an enormous fan (a fan is the *mestre-sala's* traditional hand prop) topped with a barbaric spray of ostrich feathers. Instead of a classic Grecian crown, His Black Highness wears a crown that is piled up, layer after layer, like a many-terraced wedding cake, the whole concoction, with its hooped and splayed sides, rising to the comic anticlimax in a very tiny crown, not much bigger than a topknot, riding at the summit of this coronary crescendo. In the picture, Clovis is striking a very *mestre-saleish* pose, cutting a caper, making a leg, with one shapely calf crossed over the other, one splendid slipper raised on high, as the balancing hand clutches an immense lace handkerchief, big enough for a small tablecloth.

Carnival as Discotheque

The Carioca Carnival ball is the prototype of the discotheque. Instead of the traditional etiquette and formal dance sequence of the old-fashioned European or American ball, the Cariocas have sought to achieve that stream-of-consciousness effect and that sense of terpsichorean anarchy that comes with disco dance. Instead of dance cards and partners, instead of the regular alternation of fast and slow, four-four and three-quarter time, the Cariocas (with their powerful infusion of African culture) have always fashioned public dances that were vital organic happenings unfolding according to the impulsive and spontaneous flux of the dancers' moods.

Once the downbeat is given at 11 P.M., the music never stops —except for the costume show—until the dance concludes at dawn. Like a skilful DJ in a discotheque, the conductor of the orchestra will build the excitement of the dance, step by step, tune by tune, until the dancers have reached a peak of energy and passion. Then, when he feels the moment is right, he will let them down again into moods that are cooler, bluer, and more sentimental, until they are virtually standing still and singing with that marvelous surging self-pity that is the hallmark of Latin-American sensibility. "Endless melody" was the phrase that Richard Wagner coined for this Dionysian desire to have the music match and meld totally with the tidal flux of the human soul. Endless melody is precisely what you hear at a Carioca ball as the straining trumpets and the eloquent singers and the frenzied tribal drums drive the dancers to peaks of ecstasy and then lead them down into deep declivities of soul-searching melancholy: that ravishing melancholy that "hurts so good."

The society balls are great sexual ballets of the most lavish and elegant variety, but constantly they threaten to break down into a wild headlong orgy. The final stages of an all-night ball are, in any event, apt to be pretty gross. Between the excitement of the occasion, the incitement of the music and dancing, and the effects of drink and drugs, there is no way to avoid the sometimes embarrassing, even appalling, effects of total loss of control. Women may try to cap their evening's performance by doing one last turn on top of the table or on the stage next to the band. Others sink into an erotic swoon, pressing their bodies eagerly against the arms and hands of some attractive man. Even those who have been sitting all night atop their loge Olympuses finally rouse themselves and go into action. Lovely young girls, their nut-brown bodies now glistening with sweat, line up like pony girls, each one embracing and bumping the girl before her, as photographers flash away.

The husbands and escorts, who began the evening in elegantly tailored tuxedos, now resemble a nightclub singer after an exhausting but triumphant night on the floor. Their jackets are off, their ties discarded, their shirts split to the navel. At this point, at about four o'clock in the morning, the officials would like to close down the balls because when they are prolonged beyond this time their joyous and ebullient atmosphere can turn sour and nasty.

In 1975, the last ball to be held at the opera house ended on precisely such a sorry note. In fact, what occurred that night probably had more to do with the imposing of a ban against balls at the opera house than did the official reasons, which were the restoration and preservation of the old building. Accounts of the incident vary, but apparently the imbroglio was sparked off when a woman removed the top part of her costume and a man standing beside her seized her breasts. The woman screamed and instantly another man came to her aid. The men exchanged blows and soon the entire floor of the opera house had ignited in a fierce and brutal brawl. From hands and fists, the weapons changed to bottles and chairs. People were mauled and beaten and deeply lacerated by broken glass. When the police arrived and quelled the riot, they discovered that no less than thirty people required hospital treatment. The whole melee was recorded on film but Brazil's iron censorship intervened to protect the guilty. The pictures were not destroyed: however at the offices of *O Globo* I saw a shot that was a blackmailer's dream. In a lurid burst of photoflash, one of Rio's most eminent businessmen was caught in the act of bringing down a chair squarely on another man's head.

Gay Ball

The goings-on at the society balls are decorous in comparison to what happens at the balls of the lower classes or of those daring creatures, the homosexual queens and transvestites. Dressing up in the clothes of the opposite sex is one of the oldest Carnival traditions, being a natural extension of the grand theme of social inversion and part of the universal masquerade. For the homosexuals the opportunity is golden because many of them live the rest of the year in communities that would never tolerate such blatant public exhibitionism.

The Baile das Bonecas (the "Dolls' Ball") took place in the old days at the austere Teatro João Caetano, smack in the heart of downtown Rio. It was the most notorious event of Carnival. Hustlers and male studs accosted the queens on the dance floor and often engaged in acts of public sex. The debauchery sparked scenes of sanguinary violence that sometimes concluded with murder. Finally, the authorities cracked down. Taking the view that such a popular event could not be suppressed but could be managed more discreetly, they appointed a house (the Teatro São Jose) somewhat out of the path of the tourists and foreign press and assigned dozens of special police to patrol the site. Many new regulations were promulgated, including a ban against foreign photographers. (Photos of the queens appear prominently in the Brazilian press but the generals fear that such decadence may be misconstrued by other nations and give Brazil a black eye abroad.)

The queer ball runs every night of Carnival. The queens line up in the dark street outside the theater, where they are greeted with huzzahs and mocking tributes by the crowd assembled to witness their arrival. The queens bridle, make a show of embarrassment, then turn and salute the bystanders like movie stars or burlesque queens. Some of the transvestites are minor celebrities in their own right: men who have acquired a public image that enables the spectator to recognize them and even compare how their costume this year differs from what they wore the preceding year. Once inside the desperately thronged theater, the fun takes a hectic turn. Indeed, the scene is so startling that even the most worldly-wise are taken aback.

Picture an old movie theater of the sort you'd find on 14th Street or down in the East Village in New York. The paint is peeling from the walls, the carpet is rigid with filth, the decor is dimmed with age and decrepitude. In the lobby and on the mezzanine, bright lights have been switched on as if to highlight the ghastly condition of the building. Swarms of queers are rushing about like butterflies in heat. Some of them are dressed to kill in gold lamé gowns, elaborate coiffures, masses of jewelry, makeup thick as plaster, and double rows of oversized eyelashes. Flouncing about and screaming their lungs out, they seem to be suffering from some disorder of the inner ear, like tumbling pigeons. Others are shockingly bare. Beautiful boys these, with tits of delectable contour, totally exposed because there is no law forbidding a man's baring his breast. Perhaps they are piquantly clad in workman's overalls, the big suspenders half concealing, half exposing their breasts Or perhaps they are in *tangas* that reveal everything.

Upstairs on the mezzanine, a photographer has set up an improvised studio with glaring floodlights, mirrors for primping, and stools for posing. One after another the queens come into the lights and pose singly or in couples for their picture. The photographer works feverishly behind his tripod, shouting orders to his assistants and rushing out to push the "girls" into better positions, gasping with exasperation when they jump off the stool for one last frantic look in the glass.

Meanwhile, in the theater itself, a steeply pitched, narrow shouldered old auditorium, the crowd has massed for the competition of *fantasias*, a gross and obscene parody of the great costume shows at the official balls. The temperature is stunning and the atmosphere of rank body odor and dripping sweat is oppressive. Every step you take, you are seized and fondled by swift invisible hands. Finally, you reach a seat in the balcony, but you can see nothing because everyone is standing on top of the chairs. Precariously, you poise yourself with your feet straddling the armrests of the seat. Now the stage curtains light up with spots, as the queens begin to parade, one by one.

No sooner does the first costumed figure swish into the lights than the crowd is chanting hoarsely—"*Bicha! Bicha! Bicha! Puta! Puta! Puta!*" ("Fag! Fag! Fag! Whore! Whore! Whore!"). The more they shout, the more the queens take heart. They mince, they strut, they samba. They shout back obscenities at the crowd or turn to show off their good points. Some of them have routines. They come onstage dressed like little girls rolling hoops or skipping rope. They are gamins with raked caps and knee pants. They are Harlow, Garbo, Lollobrigida. The spectacle continues for nearly an hour as the frenzy of the crowd reaches the intensity of a cock pit. Finally, the stage is threatened with engulfment.

When the spectator has glutted himself to the point of nausea, he can take one more step down into the homosexual underworld. He can reach the lowest rung by descending to the fag dance hall *par excellence*—the Club Elite.

A seamy little alley packed with young men is the site of the club. The upstairs room is already dangerously overcrowded and there are fears for the soundness of the floor, so there is much haggling at the entrance for admittance to the club. The right combination of words and *cruzeiros* works the trick and once inside and up the narrow, steeply inclined stair, you find yourself in a room filled with a dense mob of dancing men obscured in the umbral gloom. A saxophone whines with the piercing lugubriousness of a Kurt Weill melody. More stairs lead up to a small gallery backed by a bar. Seated at a table is a famous middle-aged Brazilian movie actor, drinking beer and consuming the boys before him with his eyes. One impudent lad slips down his pants and stands revealed in a scanty bikini. The fleshy face of the actor grows taut.

Below, in the snake pit, hundreds of men twist and squirm together in the gloom. The band has a black sax, a drummer, and a trumpet. Its music is all the sad songs of Carnival. There is such singing as might have been heard in the galleys or the hulks or the slave ships from Africa. It is a long cry of pain, loneliness, and purest melancholy. It is beautiful and deeply moving. It is enthralling.

I could sit here all night, listening and gazing forever. A deep homosexual affinity seems to stir at the bottom of my heart, a natural longing of man for man. An English journalist sits by my side: I hardly know him, but I begin a deep, soul-baring conversation. I speak with a bluntness and directness I can never muster when sober. I tell him that this is the heart of the artichoke, the meaning of the whole of Carnival, the last rite and confession. I tell him that we must not flinch at reporting this scene and what it means to us. He understands perfectly what I struggle to articulate through the prudery of my middle-class American mind.

The music, the singing, the twisting of tenebrous shapes on the floor below never ceases. It melds with my mood and directs my words by unconscious promptings. I remain throughout the night and finally at dawn stumble out of the stew, dead drunk but holding firmly in my mental clutch the pearl of great price which this experience has furnished me: Carnival's darkest, most strangely affecting epiphany.

Carnival Casualties

Carnival concludes not with a bang but with a whimper. As the revelry dies down, the city is left looking like an abandoned battleground. Costumed figures are huddled in doorways. Broken allegories lie in the gutter. The silence is awesome as the mosquito-spraying trucks go hissing down the gaudily decorated but deserted boulevards.

In the days when Rio was less sophisticated, it was the custom to go to the central jail on the morning of Ash Wednesday to watch the Carnival prisoners being released. It is an iron rule at Rio that anyone arrested for making mischief during Carnival must spend the duration of the festival in the lock-up, no matter when he is arrested. The spectacle of these woebegone folk trailing out of the grim old building in their tattered glad rags was relished by the wits of Rio. They called this raggle-taggle of discountenanced revelers, the Bloco of Wednesday Morning.

Though the catharsis afforded by Carnival is extolled generally as a healthy release from harmful tensions, it exacts a heavy toll in casualties. Girls become pregnant, marriages break up, jealous sweethearts take revenge, middle-aged men collapse with heart attacks, thieves and murderers have a field day—as do the assassination squads of the secret police. A festival of light and life at its most exuberant and ebullient, Carnival is also a festival of shadow and death. The most famous single document of Carnival is the film *Black Orpheus*, based on the stage production titled *Orpheus of Carnival*. Its theme is death and the struggle to undo its icy clasp on the flesh. Everywhere on the streets of Carnival there are *memento mori*, "reminders of death." Among the most familiar *fantasias* are skeletons and hangmen, ghosts and devils. A strong strain of morbidity is evident in the grand costume contest as it is likewise, at the other end of the social scale, in the sadistic imagery of whips, pitchforks, and chains familiar to maskers in the slums.

In 1976, the government issued special instructions to the police to desist from strong-arm tactics in the presence of the foreign press. Even so, there were two riots during which many people were beaten and there occurred two police-engendered murders. For the rest, 130 dead bodies, including 71 murder victims, were carried to the city morgues, and 9,545 people received first aid at hospitals during the four days from Saturday through Tuesday. This was a safe and sane Carnival compared with previous years. In 1975, the total number of casualties reached a staggering 17,000.

Some of the casualties are the result of crazy accidents, like the 200 *sambistas* in 1974 who came dancing down a dark street and suddenly found themselves barefoot in hot asphalt. Or the people who were injured when a section of the spectator stands collapsed or those who died or were injured in accidents due to drunken driving. Driving in Rio is a risky business at the best of times as cars race up to one hundred miles an hour along dimly lit, heavily congested highways that whip around blind corners and plunge through densely populated urban centers. Couple this crazy passion for speed with booze, dope, and fatigue, throw in obstructions created by ubiquitous construction projects that have converted the city streets into veritable obstacle courses and a deadly formula for traffic disasters is created.

Yet another major source of Carnival injuries is the ancient custom of hurling missiles at passers-by. This harks back to the ancient Portuguese tradition of the *entrudo*. It was once the most conspicuous single feature of Carnival. A typical missile was a small, lemon-shaped wax ball filled with perfumed water—or piss. Sand, flour, rice powder, eggshells, and rotten eggs were also employed. An edict of 1835 banned the *entrudo*, but it continued until recently in the form of the *lança-perfumes* ("ether squirters") and the barrage of confetti, serpentines, and flowers.

Another common cause of Carnival mayhem and murder is sexual jealousy. "Jealousy is the perfume of love," says a Brazilian proverb; but there is nothing very fragrant about having a liter of lye thrown in one's face by an enraged mistress or being beaten up by a brutal and drunken lover. The intrigues, assignations and amorous dalliances that are so basic a part of Carnival are no less productive of pain to the jilted partner merely because they are customary. Even that long-suffering creature, the upper-class wife, may react with unexpected fury when she picks up a Carnival magazine and sees her husband cavorting at a ball with a half-naked woman whom she recognizes as a neighbor. Calling for her chauffeur, ascending in the lift, and bursting into the offending woman's flat, the wife may have time enough to inflict serious bodily injury before she is finally pulled off her prey. In the lower classes, the fighting often involves knives and guns with inevitable and irreversible consequences. If *Black Orpheus* had been a less sentimentalized and Europeanized treatment of its theme, it would not have had to make Death an arbitrary specter haunting a doomed girl: The fell figure in the hangman's costume could have been any outraged slum bum with murder in his heart.

The deeper one penetrates the soul of Carnival, the more one encounters the specter of death. Where the vital energies are whipped up to their most violent and ecstatic peak, there is, inevitably, a dark reflex of mortality cast about the frenzied happenings. Carnival is ultimately a battle of life against death, a symbolic struggle to avert the destruction of the world. Whether the awful threat be the failure of the sun, the death of the Savior, or atomic holocaust, the sinister shadow rings the light. Life, keen life, implies always its mortal Antagonist. Hence, in the valley of the shadow the revels of Carnival flare like a beacon beating back the darkness but at the same time making the darkness more profound and mysterious.

Camera Details

As for technical details, our cameras were 3 Nikon bodies with a variety of lenses from 20 mm up to 500 mm, a motordrive and various flash guns. We mainly used Koda-chrome 25 + 65 and we found GAF 500 useful because of the interesting breakup of grain that occurs and the very high speed necessary for early evening shooting and interior shots in natural light. One or two photographs were shot on color infra-red film which changes colors to create a rather ghostly effect. We had a small tripod for the 500 mm lens but rarely used it as things moved around us so quickly we rarely had time to set it up.

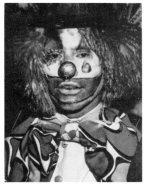

Color infrared film
1/25 at f:8
Electronic flash

Ektachrome 64
Exposure not recorded

Ektachrome 160
1/60 at f:8

Kodachrome 25
1/60 at f:8
Electronic flash

Kodachrome 25
1/60 at f:5.6
Electronic flash

Kodachrome 64
Zoom lens at 125 mm
1/60 at f:5.6
Electronic flash

Kodachrome 64
Exposure not recorded

Ektachrome 200
1/25 at f:4

Kodachrome 64
Exposure not recorded

Kodachrome 25
1/60 at f:8
Electronic flash

Kodachrome 64
1/60 at f:5.6
Electronic flash

Kodachrome 64
Zoom lens at 200 mm
(as close as I dared get)
1/25 at f:5.6
Street floodlighting

Kodachrome 25
1/60 at f:8
Electronic flash

Kodachrome 25
1/60 at f:8
Electronic flash

Kodachrome 25
Exposure not recorded

Kodachrome 64
1/60 at f:11
Electronic flash

GAF 500
1/250 at f:16
(camera shake
unintentional)

Kodachrome 25
1/60 at f:8

Shot with a shutter speed of 1 second to get the
background blur; the electronic flash was triggered
manually during the exposure to bring out the
foreground detail.
Kodachrome 25
1 second at approximately f:5.6

GAF 500
Exposure not recorded

Kodachrome 25
1/60 at f:11
Electronic flash

Kodachrome 64
1/60 at f:11
Electronic flash

Kodachrome 64
1/25 at f:16

Kodachrome 25
1/60 at f:11
Electronic flash

Ektachrome 160
Exposure not recorded

GAF 500
21 mm lens, which was necessary in this
very small room
1/60 at f:4

Infrared film
500 mm mirror lens
1/250 at f:8

Kodachrome 64
1/250 at f:5.6

Kodachrome 64
1/4 at f:8 with flash infill

Infrared film, which alters many of the colors
Exposure not recorded

Kodachrome 64
1/60 at f:11
Electronic flash

GAF 500
1/250 at f:16

Kodachrome 25
1/60 at f:11
Electronic flash

Infrared film, which turned the black cloud purple,
the red mask and toffee apple yellow, and the
grass blue and purple
Exposure not recorded

Ektachrome 200
1/25 at f:11

Kodachrome 64
500 mm mirror lens
hand held
1/250 at f:4
Floodlighting from stands

Kodachrome 64
1/15 at f:22 (to obtain blur)

Kodachrome 64
500 mm mirror lens
1/60 at f:4

Kodachrome 25
1/25 at f:11
Electronic flash

Ektachrome 160
Exposure not recorded

Kodachrome 64
1/30 at f:2.8

GAF 500
1/25 at f:11

Ektachrome 200
Exposure not recorded

GAF 500
200 mm lens with 2x converter
1/25 at f:11
A combination of this particular film and a substantially
enlarged negative brought out the dense grain patterns.

Ektachrome 200
1/8 at f:11
Under natural lighting to obtain the blurred effect

Infrared film
1/25 at f:5.6

Kodachrome 64
1/25 at f:11

Kodachrome 64
Zoom lens at 200 mm
1/25 at f:5.6

GAF 500
Exposure not recorded

GAF 500
Exposure not recorded

Kodachrome 25
1/60 at f:8
Electronic flash

Kodachrome 25
1/60 at f:8
Electronic flash

Kodachrome 25
1/60 at f:8
Electronic flash

Kodachrome 25
Exposure not recorded

Kodachrome 64
1/60 at f:4

Kodachrome 64
Exposure not recorded

Kodachrome 64
1/60 at f:11
Electronic flash

Details not recorded

Kodachrome 64
1/60 at f:8
Electronic flash infill

GAF 500
1/60 at f:2.8

Kodachrome 25
1/25 at f:11

Kodachrome 25
1/250 at f:16

GAF 500
1/500 at f:16

GAF 500
1/25 at f:11

Details not recorded

High-speed Ektachrome
1/250 at f:11

Kodachrome 64
1/25 at f:11

Kodachrome 25
Exposure not recorded

Kodachrome 64
1/15 (to produce a blurred effect) at f:16

Ektachrome 200
500 mm mirror lens with 2x converter
1/30 at f:4

Kodachrome 25
2 seconds at f:11